MAKING GOOD CHOICES

A Guide for Teens

Purvis Atkinson

ISBN: 1479119288
ISBN-13: 9781479119288
Library of Congress Control Number: 2012915249
CreateSpace Independent Publishing Platform, North Charleston, SC

Dedication

To my nephews, Jardin and Jerrell, who are living proof that when you put your mind to it, you can overcome any obstacle. I love your spirit and that you both always try to do what is right. Your persistence makes all our tomorrows brighter.

To my boyhood mentors, uncles Charles, Saul, Marcus, and T.

To Mr. Booker, my fourth-grade teacher at Sixty-First Street School in Los Angeles. You made learning fun.

To my Aunt Evelyn, whose kind words made a lifetime of difference.

To my fellow veterans, US military service members, and their families. May our country always treasure you, and may God bless you.

CONTENTS

Acknowledgements

Jerrell Francis, Robert Murphy, and Charles Bohe provided invaluable suggestions that significantly improved this book. My publishing team at CreateSpace, Jenny, Amy, Rebecca, Callie, Brianne, Maria, Sarah, and Jeannie, you are all fantastic. Thank you all so much.

Using this book

This guide contains practical things teens can do to achieve their potential. It can be used as the main text in an after-school or special summer program. This book is primarily intended for use with a teacher, parent, mentor, or tutor. However, any curious student will benefit from reading this book, working through the exercises, and completing the projects.

Each chapter addresses key life experiences that will impact a young person's future. There are many life lessons presented here. Practical recommendations to improve student life choices and outcomes are also provided.

Features

Profiles

Each chapter begins with a profile of a noteworthy American. From the First Lady to student scholars, sports heroes, and other notables, these profiles provide a list of interesting background facts. These are people from all walks of life, and all of them faced big challenges. The profiles are a segment of Americana and are intended to be inspirational and fun. Overall, these individuals, through their single-minded focus, and love of humankind have made this world a much better place. They are accomplished people. They are achievers. I hope you enjoy their stories.

Five Key Points, Projects, and Suggested Reading

Each chapter will end with a challenge, a call to action. First, you will be asked to list five key points you want to remember about what you read. Second, you will be given a project to complete. It may be simple or complex, short term or long. The point is to demonstrate what you have learned and implement it in your life.

The last thing you will see in every chapter is suggested reading. I have listed mostly biographies in this section because of their inspirational impact. Biographies also take larger-than-life people and give you insight into the not-so-impressive parts of their life. They make these individuals seem more human. In a few cases, as in chapter ten, I added a socially uplifting, inspirational book. This was done because the larger aim of *Making Good Choices* is to develop your ability to love, show empathy, and be responsible.

Notes to the Users

Students

This guide is not the total answer for all the problems in your life. It is a tool—an important tool just for you. Use it to create a fantastic future. You will need some assistance in parts of this book. Don't be too shy to ask for help from your teacher, parent, or another trusted adult. This is about making your life better. So study this book and apply the advice provided. Your progress is all that matters. Don't worry about how long it takes to work through a section. Dedicate time to the activities in the guide every day. In due time, you'll achieve your biggest dreams.

Parents

If your teen is behind in school or lacks focus, this book can help. It does not replace good parenting or a caring teacher, but with your support and interaction, this can be a tool to make learning fun for your teen. Particularly in public schools, there may not be resources to reach out to every student who stumbles. Often a teen is afraid to admit that there is a problem or is clever enough to hide a shortcoming temporarily. You and I know that every stumble not promptly addressed is an added burden to slow your teen's success. Your attention and involvement will make a world of difference.

Teachers

Thank you for your exemplary citizenship and compassion. Please use this book, along with your many other tools, to nurture your students and provide assistance to their parents. Show it at parent-teacher conferences or open houses. Put it in your library. Use it in after-school programs or summer programs. Give it to students who tutor their peers. Continue to teach how math, science, reading, and social studies are key to the wealth of vocations that are available. Keep inspiring. Keep believing.

INTRODUCTION

I came from humble beginnings. By that I mean poor, inner city, minority from a single-parent home. Yet my life has been more than I ever dreamed. I have a wonderful wife and daughter. I had a thirty-year career in the navy and rose in rank from junior enlisted to senior officer. My last two tours in the service were at the Pentagon and the White House. And I earned my college degree while in the military. After retiring from the navy, I worked in for a large corporation as a senior manager, making a very good salary.

The first eighteen years of my life were difficult and disappointing in many ways, but they also formed the basis for my impressive accomplishments as an adult. I offer this book to you, knowing full well that you may have to overcome significant hardship too. I also know that difficulty can motivate you to achieve big things. My story is not one of a kind. It is a very American mainstream story. Your story can be even grander.

My life alone isn't proof of the processes explained in the coming pages, but you will be reading about what I have learned. To validate my theories, I reviewed the lives of many extraordinary individuals. These include President Barack Obama, retired general and former secretary of state Colin Powell; the first female chief of the Cherokee Nation, Wilma Mankiller, retired general and secretary of veterans affairs Eric Shinseki; Senator Carol Mosely Braun, former US poet laureate Maya Angelou, Associate Supreme Court Justice Sonia Sotomayor, retired lieutenant general Ricardo Sanchez, political adviser Donna Brasile, former president Bill Clinton, and entertainment mogul Oprah Winfrey.

All of these accomplished people struggled with overwhelming adversity, be it poverty, mistreatment, lack of education opportunities, or prejudice. They all overcame their hardships in a spectacular fashion. Their success, like mine, is something unique to America. It is the essence of the American Dream. The idea that hard work and perseverance will ultimately yield success for anyone is true. You will see for yourself.

To more clearly show you your dream potential, I have also studied your peers. I have included what they have done and are doing to succeed in life. You will read highlights of young people around your own age who are making their dreams come true. This book provides tools that worked in the past as well as those that are working now. It can work for you.

Becoming successful is not an all-or-nothing process. It is a lifetime investment, a journey that enriches your life with every step you take. Please take this journey with me.

People who achieve long-term happiness and success are not born mentally or socially better than the rest of us. They aren't just naturally lucky, in the right place at all the right times. These people do have a single major advantage. They are *focused*. They zero in on the things that make their lives fun and full of rewards. Their energy is not wasted on a long list of things that don't actually improve their lives. They dream and plan. They work every day on achieving their dream. The result is that they become winners in life.

If you remember nothing else, remember that you must have a dream to pursue in order to achieve anything, and it is never too early to act on your dream. The sooner you identify your dream and work out a plan to achieve it, the sooner you'll be on the road to happiness. And the sooner you will develop an enduring and empowering sense of self-worth—a sense of self-respect and pride.

Use this book to help you find your dream. Use it to develop your life's plan. Learn to live your life on purpose and with meaning. Dream, plan, achieve. Keep reading.

Chapter 1

SIX GUIDING PRINCIPLES

Profile: Michelle Obama

About Mrs. Obama

Michelle Obama is the wife of President Barack Obama, a mother, and a lawyer. As the wife of the president, she is also the First Lady. Though this position is mostly ceremonial, many first ladies have also had a big influence on presidents' policies. Even before her husband was elected president, Michelle was a perfect example of the six principles in this chapter. She tries to do good, be forgiving, and keep her values in balance. She believes strongly in citizenship and teamwork, always works hard, and does her best to help others. Michelle focuses a lot of attention on helping kids, women, and military families. She is an impressive role model and does an outstanding job of showing the world all that is wonderful about our country. Here is a short profile of Michelle Obama.

Michelle LaVaughn Robinson Obama was born and raised on the Chicago South Side in a primarily black community known as South Shore. Her parents rented an apartment on the second floor of her great aunt's house. Michelle's great grandparents were slaves in South Carolina. She has one older brother, Craig Robinson, who is the head coach of men's basketball at Oregon State University. Her dad, Fraser Robinson III, who has suffered with multiple sclerosis from early adulthood, worked at a Chicago city water plant. Her mom, Marian, was a full-time homemaker until Michelle entered high school.

Michelle was raised in a working-class family. One of the values that her parents taught her and Craig was the importance of hard work. Her dad's illness took a toll over the years, but Michelle remembers that he almost never missed a day of work, even when he needed crutches to walk.

The Robinsons also stressed the importance of education. Both Michelle and Craig excelled throughout their grade school and college years. Education was so important that Michelle endured a three-hour round trip bus ride every day so she could attend Whitney Young High School. In high school as well as college, Michelle participated in minority cultural groups, academic societies, and student government.

Both Michelle and Craig received scholarships to Princeton University. After graduating law school with honors, Michelle worked at the Sidley Austin law firm as an assistant for the mayor of Chicago. She also worked as director of the nonprofit Chicago Office of Public Allies, was associate dean of students at the University of Chicago, and was director of community affairs for the University of Chicago Hospitals.

Principle I

Life is cause and effect

If you do good, admirable things come your way, and if you do bad, you get to relive that mistake over and over. This is because life is cause and effect. A positive action always brings on something favorable, and a negative action always brings on bad.

Just like in the movies, the bad guy always gets caught. Think about it: have you ever gotten away with doing something wrong? Maybe your parents didn't catch you, but I bet you still felt bad about it. You know right and wrong. It's what your parents taught you as a young child, what you learned in school, and maybe what you learned in church. When you were little and your brother told you, "Ooh, you're going to get in trouble," you knew you'd messed up. And when you tried to bribe or threaten him, you knew you were just getting into a deeper hole. But you always knew that life was cause and effect.

Some people hang on the negative. They keep digging that hole, hoping that this time they won't get caught. They make up excuses and pretend to be tough—but really they're just scared. You can make an excuse; you can claim that life isn't fair. But excuses won't get you anywhere; they don't make the bad things go away. Excuses are pretend, make-believe. You don't need endless excuses in your life. You need to own your actions.

Again, the point is that life is cause and effect. In many religions, fables, and myths, the message is if you do good, it will come back to you. This is a basic human concept, and it is also practical. Just try it the next time you have a choice to do the right thing.

No matter what, keep on making the right choice, even when it's hard, even when no one is looking. Over time you will start feeling better and better about yourself. Your parents, siblings, and friends will notice and compliment your change for the good. The power of positive actions can make miracles happen. Just one forward-looking person can change the world forever.

Life is cause and effect. It is not an issue of fairness or of good or bad luck. It's you and me working every day to do positive things. Your earnest actions will give you an advantage in life. You can concentrate on moving ahead, not covering up or fear getting caught. Yes, life is cause and effect, and when you fully embrace this idea, you'll be on the road to achieving your dreams.

Principle II

Love is forgiving, not blind

If you love people, you hold them accountable. When they do commendable things, you praise and encourage them. When they do bad things, you help them correct or take ownership of the wrong they have done. Once they have admitted to and corrected the wrongs, you should forgive them. This is the sequence of forgiveness: a wrong is committed, then that action is corrected, and then the victim of the wrong forgives the person who hurt him or her.

The old saying "love is blind" is just not true. That saying is often used as an excuse to try to ignore bad behavior. Claiming that something bad was done for love is just a way to try to make something bad seem okay. So if you love someone who is racist, for example, it's okay to love them and not address their prejudice. If it's your mom, dad, brother, or sister, you ignore the problem? The only issue is that that last sentence is wrong. You and I have to address wrongdoing for what it is and no matter who does it.

In principle one, you learned an important lesson that is always true: life is cause and effect. You can't walk away from the truth, because it will follow you to the ends of the earth like a lost puppy. "Love is blind" is a poison that has been fed to us like rotten vegetables for dinner. The more you take this poison, the worse off you'll be. It can only hurt you and those you love.

The belief that you can love someone no matter what isn't really about love at all. Perhaps this idea was intended to place love of family above all else, and in this sense, it is compassionate but hands-off. It does not make the world or the family better; it makes anything acceptable. But saying that love is *forgiving* and not blind adds a sense of responsibility. If you look at love in this way, you say, "Though I love you, I recognize when you are wrong, and it is my responsibility to help you take the right action. I will not turn a blind eye, because I love you. I will stand behind you and help guide you. If you try to change your bad conduct, I will forgive you. I do this because I love you and want you to be the best person you can be. Because I love you, I am concerned about your welfare. Because I love you, I will not close my eyes when you hurt yourself or hurt someone else. I do this because love is nurturing and forgiving."

Principle III

What you value guides your life

Are your values anchors or trampolines? Do they weigh you down, keeping you from moving up, or do they spring you up toward the heavens. Determining what really matters in your life should be easy. Love and friendship are things you cannot buy; they are priceless. Happiness and peace of mind are things some people search their whole life to find, and some never find them. Being a first-rate person—honest, trustworthy, reliable, and humane—is not only for those who are rich. These traits are what we all have or should have.

Most of us also value physical possessions and lots of money. This is understandable, because about 98 percent of the people in the United States are from working class families. You and I want more. You may believe that the high life is mostly about money and that those other nice things, like love and friendship, come with our good-fortune limousine. But this is the truth: if you and I value love, friendship, truth, honesty, and hard work, monetary wealth can come as a by-product of those values.

For example, Bill Gates was born middle class and is now one of the richest people in the world, thanks to his values, vision, and a company he started called Microsoft. Bill Clinton was raised by his poor mom; he later became the forty-second president of the United States and a millionaire. Oprah Winfrey grew up in poverty and had a very difficult childhood, but she overcame these hardships. Thanks to her values and determination, she is now a billionaire who owns a television network and who is constantly helping others improve their lives. Look at these websites to see for yourself: **www.gatesfoundation.org, www. clintonglobalinitiative.org, www.oprah.com**.

The list of people who have set up organizations to help others, like the Boys and Girls Clubs and Big Brothers Big Sisters, is very long—longer than you can imagine. Many of these people could have used their energy solely to increase their own personal wealth, but money was not the only thing they valued. For these people and the millions and millions of volunteers who help run charitable organizations, what they value above money is the opportunity to give to others so that their lives are improved. What these people value above money is love and friendship, and the simple joy of sharing humanity with a needy stranger.

Work to figure out how to balance what you value with your desire for possessions. I trust that you will find that love of humankind and nature are two of your top priorities. True wealth is priceless. Fill your life with values that are trampolines, and you will always be reaching for the heavens.

Principle IV

Good citizenship matters

You and I have an obligation as human beings to help one another. Some people only care about themselves. These are lonely, unloved souls. Humans are social animals who do not survive well on our own. You need compassion and companionship, not only to survive, but to thrive. Some believe that the saying "good fences build good neighbors" is not just a plea for occasional privacy but a way of life. But isolation is a type of punishment, not a way of life. Isolation is not a way to survive and keep your sanity.

Good citizenship is not only caring about others; it is also respecting the rights of others. It is doing your duty for your community and recognizing you are your brother's and sister's keeper. At the signing of the Declaration of Independence in 1776, Benjamin Franklin said, "We must all hang together or we will assuredly hang separately." Though this saying had a very specific meaning for the time, it is still true today, because you are stronger when you work together with others. You can apply this to the quest for equal rights, to increasing charity, or to improving education and the environment. It works for any big issue people must come together to solve. The responsibility of citizenship is far reaching, but it is also an extension of our role in our own families.

So, what are some of the things that good citizens do? Well, they obey the law. They report crimes. They help those in need. They work to make their community better by volunteering and setting excellent examples. When they are eighteen or older, they exercise their right and responsibility to vote. By voting, you choose politicians to run our government, and they can approve changes to our laws.

Some of our very best citizens serve in the military, on police forces, in fire departments, as teachers, and in charitable organizations. But anyone can and should be a stellar citizen, regardless of his or her age or occupation. To be a top-notch citizen, you have to care and to act to help others.

Being an admirable citizen can be hard. It may require trying to help people you don't really know or who are different from you. Helping someone you don't know is an act of friendship, but it's also a real act of citizenship. Being a good citizen may require that you not only give your time but also your money. Please note that one does not replace the other; you have to give *both*.

Becoming an accomplished citizen may require you to take a big risk. Those who join our military, police forces, and fire departments risk their lives. Most of us are not willing to do this. These brave risk takers deserve our utmost respect.

Citizenship is about standing up for what is right. If you are not willing to stand up for yourself and others, then how are you entitled to all the benefits that past splendid citizens have earned for you? Everyone has to earn their place in society. It is the price of freedom, and it's called "citizenship."

Principle V

Life is a team sport

As I said earlier, you cannot exist by yourself. You actually enjoy being needed. If a friend is picking a soccer team, you want to be chosen. If your family is going on a trip, you expect to be taken along. If you're in the school play, you expect your parents to come and see you. Life has little meaning for us unless someone else is paying attention to us. You thrive on attention. That same "watch me" you yelled to Mommy and Daddy so many times when you were a little kid is an expression of your need for others. Whether or not you admit it, you want to be part of the team.

There is power and excitement in numbers, a feeling of safety and of comfort. The need to belong is what love is all about. The desire to win acceptance can drive us to do good or bad things. So it's not just sports-team acceptance that you and I want; it goes deeper. It is almost like breathing; if it is taken away, you cannot survive. No one wants to be all alone; it scares us and can harm us. You and I need to be part of a family, team, and community.

Who you are has a lot to do with who you associate with. So surround yourself with admirable people. If friends or family run into problems, help them do the right thing. Keep your team strong by doing your best and encouraging your teammates to do their best. Your role in your family, team, and community is to be a go-to person—the one everyone counts on to come through when the going gets tough. In this way you win in life, and no one is hurt.

Successful people in all walks of life rely on teamwork. They realize they cannot be their best unless they have a top-notch team around them. You hear it time and again in every success story: a parent, sibling, friend, teacher, coworker, or sometimes even a total stranger helps the successful person on their path to success. Nobody succeeds by themselves; it is not possible. Whether you know it or not, there is always a helping hand reaching out to you. Do yourself a favor: grab that hand and be grateful.

Teambuilding is important. Everyone on your team will falter and require help at times; everyone has a bad day. Your job is to help guide your team to success. Learn to pay attention and to listen to your teammates. In this way you will be ready to step in as needed until things are okay. Like a substitute who comes into the game when someone is injured or in foul trouble, you should be there for you family and community. You should respect everyone for their talents and encourage them to do their best. By working together as a team, with everyone doing their best, you can do almost anything. Find your talent, develop it, and join the roster!

Principle VI

Good things come to those who work

You get out of life what you put into it. As you get older, you will understand that a good outcome from cause and effect, forgiveness, the right values, good citizenship, and the joy of teamwork comes as a result of how hard you have worked to succeed. Sincerity of effort matters like an open mind and a loving heart. The rewards are worth more than gold.

There is something that you do well. By working hard to improve on your natural talent, you can be your best. The first task is to find out what your talent is. I will spend a whole chapter on helping you find and develop your talent. The second step is to take action. Develop a plan, give yourself a realistic timeline to work your plan, and then give it 100 percent. A reasonable timeline for a plan is one to five years. It is also normal to adjust your plan as you go, as you get new or better information about the time needed to achieve your goal. Start thinking long term when it comes to your future.

If you were to interview several successful people, you'd likely discover that, though they may mention the word *luck*, they actually put in a lot of work before their opportunity "miraculously appeared." Remember the saying about things that are "too good to be true." You have to work to get ahead. It's not about luck. Make no mistake about it, work trumps luck every time. Your odds improve if you simply apply yourself to a well-developed plan. So don't be afraid to work hard and to find joy in your work. You'll be surprised by the excellent things that come your way.

List five key points you want to remember from this chapter:

1.

2.

3.

4.

5.

Projects

Interview one of your parents, and write a short biography. Here are some sample questions to ask. You can add to or take away any questions you choose.

    a. Where were you born?

    b. How many brothers and sisters do you have?

    c. Where did you live growing up?

    d. Who was your best friend when you were a kid? Why?

    e. Who was your favorite teacher? Why?

    f. What was your best subject in school?

    g. What do you value most in life?

Suggested Reading

Sonia Sotomayor: Supreme Court Justice by Carmen T. Bernier-Grand

Chapter 2

OUR COUNTRY

Profile: Kyla Ross

About Kyla

Professional championships provide an athlete with more money, but the victories are seldom truly international. Many professional athletes are not world champions. Those who perform well at the Olympics are exceptions. There you are part of something grander: you represent a whole country, and you compete with the best in the world. A gold medal is something each athlete cherishes individually and shares with millions. The Olympics also represent the highest values of sportsmanship and individual integrity. For a few weeks, every couple of years, the hopes and dreams of many nations rest on the shoulders of a few thousand athletes. These competitors have worked diligently for many years to get to that point. That is Kyla's story, and it's why many admire and cheer for her.

Kyla Ross was born in 1996 in Honolulu, Hawaii. She is the oldest of three children born to Jason and Kiana Ross. Kyla's family is a perfect example of American diversity and success. Her dad, a former minor league baseball player, is probably where she inherited her impressive athletic ability. Her grandparents on her father's side of the family are African American and Japanese. Washington Ross, her granddad, is a retired army master sergeant. Kyla's mom's parents are Filipino and Puerto Rican.

Kyla and her Filipino grandmother, Dianna Mascolo, were kindred spirits. She may have been the first to realize Kyla's star potential. Family members considered Kyla and her grandmother to be very much alike—both had tremendous energy and were always active. In 2010 Dianna passed away, forever changing Kyla's life. Even today, as a tribute to her grandmother, Kyla wears Dianna's diamond earrings during competitions. It is a way to hold on to that bond between them.

Kyla's gymnastic career began early. According to her mom, Kiana, "She was born with muscles. We would go to the park and everyone would say, 'Whose baby is on top that jungle gym?'"

By the age of three, when the family had moved to Greenville, South Carolina, Kyla began training at the Greenville Gymnastics Training Center. Within two years, she had made significant progress. She began competing at age five. Even though she was tiny compared with the older kids, she held her own.

For the past ten years, Kyla has lived in Aliso Viejo, California, and trained at Gym-Max Gymnastics. She rapidly progressed through the lower levels of competition, winning gold and silver medals in almost every championship. She was selected for the Junior US National Team in 2008. While only fifteen and practicing her gymnastic routines thirty to thirty-five hours a week, Kyla was selected for the USA 2012 Olympic Team. That team, The Fierce Five, was the first U.S. women's gymnastic team to win the gold medal since July 1996. That's not bad for her first Olympic competition.

Our Country's Foundation

What would become the United States was just a random group of territories conquered by the European superpowers from the 1400s through 1600s. This jumble of colonies was merely a source of goods, manpower, and exotic adventure stories. Who would have guessed that this so-called land of primitives would someday grow to become one of the most powerful nations in history? Who would have guessed that this hodgepodge of Dutch, Portuguese, Spanish, British, and French business interests would rise up against the mightiest nations of that time, declare its independence, and succeed?

This unlikely, unbelievable story is the humble and inspiring tale of our heritage. Our legacy is the dreams, work ethic, and spirit of freedom that early citizens of the United States had. Both as individuals and as a nation, we Americans have stood up for ourselves and chased our dreams. Freedom, dreams, and hard work are our foundation.

The first Europeans to explore America came in search of riches, which they were prepared to take by force if needed. Their explorations were funded by their kings, queens, and business groups. The people who later settled in the United States were a more diverse group. Some were the king's cohorts–that is, rich business people. Their main interest was to fill their pockets with more wealth. Yet the vast majority of colonists were average to poor people who longed for religious freedom and the opportunity to start their lives anew. It is important to separate these two groups. It is just as important to realize that a nation must have both to grow a prosperous society for all.

What these first settlers had in common was their willingness to take a calculated risk. They were optimists willing to try almost anything to improve their lives. They were not mere gamblers trying their luck with a roll of the dice. They were blessed, as it were, to have the opportunity to work hard to experience what came to be known as the American Dream.

The greatness of the United States is anchored in its core documents: the Declaration of Independence and the Constitution. The first document boldly announced to the world that we were a free people. The second one established our moral and legal basis for existing. The process of amendments adds checks and balances to the Constitution, making it a precious, living treasure that grows in goodness and importance over time.

Out of Many, One

So there you have it. The sometimes very difficult but ultimately successful union of a ragtag group of Native Americans, Africans, and Europeans gave birth to a remarkable nation. Over time, others would come from South America, Asia, and other far-away lands. They too would add to the legacy of greatness in "the land of opportunity." They too would struggle for acceptance but in the end would earn the right to be citizens of the United States of America. "Out of many, one" is a prophetic and wonderfully true quotation.

You may wonder where this quotation came from. In 1776 artist Pierre Eugene du Simitiere, a Swiss immigrant, was employed by the Continental Congress to design the first United States seal. Though some of his ideas were not used, his suggestion for the United Sates motto, "Out of many, one" (in Latin, *E Pluribus Unum*), was adopted. There is no other phrase that so completely describes what the United States symbolizes to us and the rest of the world. In three Latin words, Pierre captured the hopes and dreams of the American people then and now. The United States began as a nation of Native Americans and immigrants. This theme of immigrant acceptance and prosperity has been repeated with immense pride for generations. What it means is that, no matter where you come from, you can find freedom and opportunity here.

America is much more than a nation of one dominant race with any number of immigrant outsiders. It is open to the world, welcoming citizens from all nations and economic backgrounds. This country is made strong by all the different people who have come here over time—some with nothing but hopes and dreams.

In actual practice, America has struggled with applying this motto of acceptance to all its citizens and immigrants. We are not a nation of angels, but of people who make mistakes and learn from those mistakes. The founding fathers set the ideals for this best-of-all-worlds very high. You and I have to work every day to be as fair and as understanding as our Constitution requires, to be that shining example of freedom, tolerance, and fair play.

But the fantastic news is that the more you work to become all that you can be, the better you make the United States and the world. The constant struggle for freedom for all is both noble and worth every minute of effort.

"Out of many, one" not only unites us, it also inspires. It is an expression of love and acceptance, and it is a foundational building block of one of the most influential nations on earth.

Changes for the Better

You can always improve. That is why you can wake up filled with hope every morning. It is why you and I can believe with all our hearts that dreams really do come true. The power of change to enhance our lives is part of how we think and live. Change for the better is a positive notion. Always think of change as a second chance to get it right, to improve and grow. You and I are fortunate to embrace change while others may fear it. Our outlook is positive because we live in a wonderful and hopeful place, the land of endless opportunity, the United States.

The governing document for our country, the Constitution, is a perfect reflection of what is commendable and right about the United States. It is a work in progress. It is not sacred and untouchable. Even in its initial state, there were ten amendments to further clarify the rights of citizens. That process has continued through time; now there are twenty-seven amendments. The fact that the Constitution can be amended is a testament to the wisdom of our founders. They knew that they did not create the perfect document, though it may have been the very best they could produce at the time. But they also understood that humankind would understand more and more about this world and ourselves. The amendment process made it possible for us to adjust to our increased understanding—our enlightenment—gained over time.

What is truly amazing is that regardless of the initial influence of business and limited representation, what came forth was a representative yet timeless democratic document. How fantastic is that?! The most wonderful gift the founders gave us was the means to change things, to reform. Both as a country and as individual citizens, change for the better is what we should be about.

Of course, there is still a ways to go, and that is where you come in. It is your responsibility, your duty, to give of yourself to improve society. Your legacy to future generations is a higher quality life. You have all the tools you need to make that happen. Make your life noteworthy by dedicating yourself to the enhancement of humankind. Make changes for the better.

Integrity

Integrity is a belief in and practice of certain valued principles. It includes the six principles outlines in chapter one, but it is centered on the concepts of truth, honor, honesty, and reliability. Integrity is "taking the high road." When faced with a choice of doing the wrong thing because it seems quick and easy or doing the right thing, you should do what is right. That is the high road. If your life is full of shortcuts and easy solutions, you are likely not living with integrity. Your victories will be shallow, and your disappointments will seem endless.

Integrity is something that you first learn to appreciate in others, such as the people you have come to rely on: your parents, teachers, and true friends. When you need them, they are always there to help and guide you. If there were no people of integrity in your life, you'd be lost and alone, like the sole survivor on an unknown island.

The founding fathers took it as a given that each person is a person of integrity and as such has human rights and citizenship. Each was assumed to be fair in business dealings and respectful of others rights and property. They believed in an agreed system of shared values, and trusted each other to keep his or her word. Basically they assumed everyone would exercise integrity. Some are fascinated with the idea that Americans are independent individuals. Independence is important, but when you are choosing friends, I suggest you make integrity one of your top criteria. A friend without integrity is not much of a friend.

One of the most cherished things you can have is others' belief in your integrity. In other words, can you be trusted. No amount of money or education can replace a loss of integrity.

Be a person of integrity. This too is hard work, but worth it.

Individual Responsibility

To be a person of integrity, take ownership of your choices. Take responsibility for what you do and say. If you make a choice, you own the outcome—good or bad. One very American term is the pioneer spirit. This refers to the mindset and motivation that causes you to set out on your own to work day and night for a life that surpasses your dreams. Our country's tradition is one of taking action, owning responsibility for our destiny, and accepting responsibility for our family's welfare. In the old West, especially, a man's and a woman's fortune was determined by that person's motivation. The people of the old West were law abiding, valued fairness, accepted responsibility, and often had values based on religious principles.

Religion is an important component of many of our lives. (Note that there are many splendid people who may not share my or your specific religious beliefs.) Though I will not comment on the goodness of any particular religion, I will say that one of the pillars of most religions is individual responsibility—the concept that we are accountable for our actions, that we have free will to do what is right. The belief in karma is based on individuals making good or bad choices and reaping the rewards or suffering the consequences of those actions. Do you remember cause and effect? If you are responsible in your actions, both the cause and the effect will be positive.

Individual responsibility is about taking action. Don't let anyone lead you astray and keep you from being responsible and trustworthy. And don't just sit and wait for others to do your share. Life is not about waiting for the good Samaritan to come knocking at your door. No matter how bad your life is, you still have the responsibility to take action; you still have individual responsibility. The cycle of sit, wait, feel bad, and eventually someone helps is a dead end. That is not living; it is the waste of a life. Avoid this cycle by taking action; taking responsibility.

Own and direct your destiny. Individual responsibility requires that you stand up for yourself and take charge of your life.

Breaking news, good news! Your life is your responsibility.

Choices

As I have discussed our country's beginnings, the power of positive change, integrity, and individual responsibility, the common thread is that of *choices*. Our founding fathers bravely stepped up and produced a governing document that gave hope to the common citizen. At that time, the level of freedom and independence guaranteed to the common person was not equaled anywhere in the world. They made the choice to create a new model of governance. It was based on the best Europe had to offer. But it went further, and the evidence of its impact is reflected in the number of immigrants who still believe that the United States is their best hope. Our founders made the hard choices—those best for all the people of this nation. They set the tone for cooperative change, individual responsibility, and pride. You and I cannot back down from our responsibility to make our own best choices for ourselves and the common good.

The saying "It's not where you start but where you finish that counts" is something every American should take to heart. It's never too late to make a life changing bold choice. It is our obligation to leave a legacy of inspiration and accomplishment to those who come after us and those who look up to us. The oldest American to earn his high school diploma was Gustava Bennett Burrus; he did it at age ninety-seven. This is an example of how dreams acted upon, at any time, can become true in this country.

In many places, you are destined to the fate of your father or mother, but that is not so in the United States. If your father's life is one of wealth and splendor, congratulations. If it is a life of struggle and squalor, well, okay. Neither situation is the final word on where your life will go. You have the choice to change for the better.

You have a choice and an opportunity to be all that you can be. In American, the rich have choices, but so do average workers and the poor. You can determine your own fate. It's all a matter of how hard concerned and motivated citizens, like you, are willing to work for change. It is your choice, and in order to realize such an important choice, you have to act on it. You have to do something positive and not settle for the way things are or always have been.

You always have choices. Sometimes it's as simple as choosing right over wrong. Perhaps it's way too easy to choose wrong— or it's very complicated not to. Perhaps you feel that you don't really have a choice, that any path you take leads to the same dead end. Stop. It's not too complicated. If you see a dead end, turn around. You do have a choice. Yes, you are in charge of your life.

Yes, you have the choice to consistently make good choices. So work everyday to make good choices. This will pay now and in the future, so why cheat yourself out of the triumph you deserve? You are not a victim, and you don't need to waste time with excuses. Live on purpose. Get the results you want by making right choices. The consequences of bad choices and hurtful decisions need not weigh you down. It's just that simple.

List five key points you want to remember from this chapter:

1.

2.

3.

4.

5.

Projects

1. Find a copy of the Constitution for your grade level, and read all of it. Don't forget the amendments.

2. Read and memorize the Preamble to the Constitution.

3. Pick one or two topics to discuss with your parents, brother or sister, or friends.

Suggested Reading

Native American Tales and Legends, edited by Allan A. Macfarlan

Chapter 3

FAMILY AND FRIENDS

Profile: William and Jada Smith Family

About the Smith Family

What is a family? Is it the ideal of a mom and dad, a son and daughter all living in a nice four-bedroom house with a pretty white fence? Is it something more than the names on a marriage or birth certificate? Is the family relationship built on love and caring, or is it just a duty, a job for parents and children? In this chapter, we'll look at family and other relationships.

Some of the things you know about these relationships are true, while some are just myths, not based on anything real. The Smith family is both unique and ideal in many ways. What you will see in their story is that family relationships may not be what you experience every day, yet they are nurturing and loving all the same.

Both Will and Jada Smith were raised on the East Coast in middle-class families. Will's father repaired refrigerators, and his mom was a school administrator. Jada's dad ran a construction company, and her mother was the head nurse in an inner-city clinic. While Jada's parents divorced shortly after she was born, Will's parents separated when he was thirteen. Will and Jada were raised in loving families that nurtured their development as strong and positive individuals.

Both Will and Jada were highly motivated and focused. They did well in school. Jada was also fortunate in that her grandmother enjoyed the arts and shared that love with her. Jada initially went to college in North Carolina, while Will, though he did do well on his Scholastic Aptitude Test, declined his chance to go to college.

They both pursued their dreams. Will became a rapper with his best friend, Jeffrey Townes "DJ Jazzy Jeff." Jada went to Hollywood to start her acting career. While Will enjoyed high praise and popularity as a rapper, his big break came in television with the show *The Fresh Prince of Bel-Air*. From that show, he went on to become a number-one box-office attraction with notable movies, such as *I Robot*, the *Men in Black* series, and *The Pursuit of Happiness*.

Jada gained television fame as a star in *A Different World* and a show she produced called *Hawthorne*, whose main character may have been inspired by her mother. Jada's movie blockbusters include *The Nutty Professor*, *Bamboozled*, *Scream 2*, *Set It Off*, and *The Matrix Reloaded*.

Will and Jada have two children, Jaden and Willow, who both have impressive careers in acting and music, respectively. Will has another son, Trey, who is currently in college and plays wide receiver for his college football team.

Will and Jada believe strongly in giving back to their community. Their nonprofit organization, The Will and Jada Smith Family Foundation, helps inner-city families. They believe in families helping families and set an excellent example.

Parents

So, the old joke goes, "Parents, you can't live with them and you can't live without them." Of course, the best jokes have some element of truth. Being a parent is hard work, and sometimes it involves a lot of trial and error. There is no magic book for every parent to read to raise every child. If only life were that easy. Every child is different; every child is a wonderful and unique challenge. Hats off to your parents for taking on the challenge.

Parents are not children. If they were, they would have a lot less to offer you. Their role is to teach you life lessons, good conduct, and to help you realize your goals. They guide and teach you, not as peers but as mentors. This is in the hope that, one day you are able to take off on your own as an independent and productive person.

Take what you have—no matter how little—and make the best of it. Take ownership of your family and your actions, warts and all. Everyone in your family has a place and a role. Respect everyone, and start where you are with improving your life. Don't waste time wishing other circumstances on your family. Give everyone credit for what they do. Take positive action to change; improve the circumstances that require change in whatever way you can. Be patient, focused, forgiving, and hard working.

There are a lot of scenarios that meet the criteria of a loving family. Some families have moms and dads, while others have only one parent. Some of us are adopted or have foster parents. As long as you have at least one adult who loves you and cares for you, you'll be okay. But this is not to say that growing up in a single-parent home is easy. Since there is only one person providing money, a lack of it can be a source of shame and frustration. Take those feelings and use them to find constructive solutions. Help ease the burdens on the parent who loves you. If you apply yourself, you can help make many things better for your family.

Principle two in chapter one is "Love is forgiving, not blind." This is especially true when it comes to our family. It is a valuable lesson that will help you understand and help your parents. The power to forgive is a mighty tool. It will make you stronger than you ever knew you could be. It will ease your mind and calm your spirit.

It takes time and effort to learn to forgive. This is a lesson that you must master before you can go on happily with your life. You can gain fame and money, but the burden of hate can weigh you down and infect your relationship with others—unless you learn to forgive. So when you feel hurt, take a moment, a timeout. Take a deep breath, relax. Figure out how you can improve the situation. Learn to forgive the person that wronged you. When you solve problems in positive ways, you and those you love win.

Walk a Mile...

Putting yourself in the other person's position is called empathy. The saying "walk a mile in the other person's shoes" means that if you put yourself in the same situation as another person, you can appreciate why they do what they do. This is more than asking him how he feels or why she did what she did. It requires that you actually experience what the other person is going through. It is a way of getting outside of your comfort zone and your point of view. It requires that you open your eyes to new feelings and perspectives—and that you open your heart.

A splendid way to start the forgiveness process is to learn to empathize. Put yourself in your parent's or sibling's shoes. Try to understand how they came to the choices they made. Also try to figure out how you can help them. You might be surprised. True empathy requires that you actually change your perspective enough to want to find ways to help.

Experiencing some problems in your life is normal. Some of your problems can be learning experiences. From these, you come out on the other side with an improved understanding of how to relate to others. You gain perspective on what is important and what isn't. Truly, adversity is our teacher.

For example, if your parents have to work extra hours just to provide for your family, maybe they deserve a break. Granted, it hurts when you don't get your fair share of attention. Regardless of the reason, it's painful when your parents don't have time for you. This is where your ability to empathize comes in. Try to see through your parents eyes. What options do your parents have? They may be working just to make ends meet, putting food on the table, and providing shelter for your family. They may just want you to be better off. Maybe they are working hard to earn money for your college education or to make sure you get the music lessons you want so badly.

Is there anything you can do to help them? If nothing else, you can show your appreciation by taking the initiative to do chores before you are asked. And what about remembering to show your gratitude by offering a few kind words of thanks and understanding?

Maybe as you get more skilled at this empathy thing, you can take a look at what your parents are working to achieve. See where you fit in and, most importantly, how you can help.

Stand Up for Yourself

One of the challenges of growing up is earning the respect of others. One way to do that is to learn to stand up on your own. When you feel as though someone wants to hurt you or if someone has hurt you, your first reaction may be to become mad, scared, or withdrawn. These responses are normal, but you also need to take a positive action.

In this situation, think before you react. I know that is easier said than done when your blood is boiling and you're seeing red. Stop. Think through your choices, and pick an option that helps, instead of getting yourself into an even deeper mess. It is important that you don't cause more trouble, but it is also important that you take some positive action. You don't want this situation to be repeated. You want to make an intelligent stand. If it's family or friends who hurt you, let them know that you don't want to be treated that way anymore. If it is a situation outside of your family, make sure you let your parents or teacher know—or even the police, if needed.

Peers add another level of pressure that can make it difficult to see the right path. You know doing wrong or hurting other people to get someone else to like you is never an acceptable idea. Back away from so-called friends who want you to lie, bully, or engage in anything illegal. Nothing worthwhile comes from any of these actions, and there's nothing fun about having a juvenile record. Sometimes your peers can make doing the wrong things seem right. But this is real life, and what is wrong is just wrong.

The challenge of growing up is to be able to stand on your own and make good choices. The benefit of a good choice can be immediate. For example, you choose not to take drugs; therefore you do not put yourself in a position where the police may be involved. By making this more suitable choice, you avoided possible arrest or getting expelled from school.

Remember, you will always have to pay for your bad choices. Though most mistakes can be overcome, it's to your advantage not to make serious mistakes in the first place. Most people want to see you succeed. Everyone loves a story of redemption and triumph. You have to be brave. Stand up and tell that success story-the story of your life.

Role Models and Mentors

You need role models and mentors. My uncles and my fourth-grade science teacher were my mentors and role models. I would have been lost without them. I am both fortunate and thankful for their caring guidance.

A role model is someone you look up to and want to be like. Athletes are often picked as role models, but some of them don't deserve that important title. A mentor has to be someone you can trust to lead you in the right direction. This is someone you can go to for help with homework, personal problems, or career advice. You should surround yourself with role models and mentors of good character. Follow their positive lead. There are people in your family, neighborhood, school, church, etc., who are splendid people to look to for guidance. Your family is an excellent place to start your search for people of compassion and integrity who will help you.

When choosing a role model or mentor, base your decision on whether or not he or she is caring, giving, and respectable. That's why a parent or teacher may be a good role model. Set your standards very high. One test for picking role models is to notice what they say and do. If they are always saying or doing things that make other people feel bad, then keep looking for a better model. Nobody's perfect, and it's okay if your mentor or role model is not perfect. He or she should be honest and positive. Pick someone who may not be right all the time but who tries to do the right thing all the time.

A role model could also be someone you admire but don't have a personal relationship with. This could be your school principal or even the President of the United States. However, a mentoring relationship is more personal and interactive. A mentor is someone you know and can frequently go to for advice. Mentors are life-choice guides in specific situations. They can explain how the world works, about school and friends, or planning for your future. They can be the person you go to when you just need someone to listen.

Some organizations offer mentors. These include Boys and Girls Club, Big Brothers Big Sisters, sororities, fraternities, and many businesses. You may have more choices than you know.

Remember that if an issue develops with a role model or mentor, you should discuss it with your parents or another trusted adult. You may need to make a change, but that's okay. There are lots of excellent people available and willing to help guide you to success. Start looking for your mentors and role models today.

Helping Others

Most cultures consider helping others a basic human responsibility. In ancient Africa, where the first civilizations appeared, family and community were closely linked. Everyone had a role, a place of value in society. No one was left on their own to fend for themselves. Today, some people confuse helping others with merely giving handouts. When you help someone who is less fortunate it is an act of compassion. It is human and good for your soul. Everyone has value, regardless of ethnicity, education, religion, wealth, or the past that they have overcome.

Working together and helping others makes our society stronger. Throughout history, it has always been that way. You are at your best when you reach out to others. You find yourself in conflict, with your values, when you invent reasons to believe you are superior to anyone else. You are in harmony, with your conscience, when you are helping others anywhere in the world.

Consider Ben Franklin's quote in chapter 1, "We must all hang together or we will assuredly hang separately." This statement was made during a critical time in the founding of our democracy. The idea was not "fend for yourself and keep your pockets full," but band together, and achieve the greatest gift to humankind: freedom.

In practical terms, if you help someone—be it a classmate who does not have anything for lunch or who needs help with solving a math problem—you make the world a better place. If you have done something to help a hungry person or help educate someone, you should feel proud. If you are helping someone survive another day or improving that person's life in some way, how can that be considered anything other than wonderful?

List five key points you want to remember from this chapter:

1.

2.

3.

4.

5.

Projects

1. Write down who you'd like to ask to be your mentor and why.

2. Write down three people who are your role models, and describe why you chose them.

3. Realizing that mentors and role models change as we get older, and our needs change, explain why you might be changing your current mentors and role models.

Reading Suggestions

American Women Who Shaped American History by Deborah Felder

Chapter 4

WHAT IS HAPPINESS?

Profile: Arne Duncan

About Arne Duncan

Few occupations are as praiseworthy as that of educator. I think very highly of those who help us find the key to open the door to our future. As the secretary of education, Arne Duncan is the highest-ranking educator in the United States. He provides guidance and support to about 100 million students and six million teachers. When President Obama appointed Arne to his position, he accepted the job of his dreams. All of his life, he has worked in education. If true happiness is family, friends, and finding your calling, then Arne knows what it is to be happy many times over. His work has made his hometown of Chicago and the United States better and more hopeful places. Here's his story.

Arne Duncan was raised in a middle-class family with a rich tradition of service to the community. His mother, Sue, tutored African American boys and girls in the Kenwood area of South Chicago. She continued her inspired work despite threats on her life from a few who did not want her there. In the early 1960s, she established the Sue Duncan Children's Center, working out of local churches, and later an elementary school. Arne spent a lot of his free time helping his mother tutor students. His father, Starkey, was a psychology professor at the University of Chicago.

Arne's parents had a profound influence on him. He discovered early in life that his calling was to help others, particularly those who did not have the means to help themselves. He did very well in high school and college, graduating from Harvard University with the highest honors. After college and a short stint in Australia playing basketball, Arne went back to Chicago. There he accepted a job as the director of the Ariel Education Initiative. At Ariel he provided programs and long-term mentoring for inner-city kids in some of the worst-performing schools in Chicago.

Arne's achievements at Ariel brought him notoriety as well as an appointment as the deputy chief of staff for Chicago Public Schools. He was later selected by the mayor to serve as the chief executive officer of Chicago Public Schools. In this extremely difficult job, Arne continued to make a difference. His leadership resulted in better test scores for students, increased school safety, and greater community pride. As US Secretary of Education, his performance has been impressive. One of his most well-known initiatives is Race to the Top, which encourages states to propose new solutions to providing effective education.

If true happiness is helping others succeed, Arne Duncan may be the happiest guy in the United States.

Family

Happiness is a loving family. Your life begins and ends with family. They are the ones who know you best and love you the most. Navigating through family relationships puzzles all of us at times. But it is also true that our family is where we learn about fairness, individual differences, and sharing. As in the social groups of all animals, the family is where you learn how to survive. Most of all, our families teach us to love and how warm and complete it makes us feel.

At best, most families are like buildings under construction, so not everything is in place. There are times when it doesn't look like much, but with hard work, day after day, a solid structure takes shape. To build a sturdy house or family, everyone has to pitch in. Sitting on the curb and watching everyone else work makes construction take longer. Members of your family may get upset with you if you are not doing your share of the work.

Life is a team sport, and you must do your share. Your family is the home team; they are the ones you are cheering for and who are cheering for you. It is important to suit up every day and give your best. You must try, even when you don't feel like it. You'll be surprised how quickly your mood can change for the better once you get involved.

As you are doing your part to build that sturdy house, you will learn about trust and respect. You won't think twice about climbing a ladder to fix a problem on the roof if you know your sibling is holding the base of the ladder so you don't fall. You'll learn that maybe you're not the best painter, but your sister does a terrific job, and that's okay.

In a family, everyone has a role and a place. This is true of our biological family, but it is also true of our community and the world at large.

Community

Happiness is a loving community. There is a saying credited to ancient African society: "It takes a village to raise a child." This saying speaks to the heart of what our community can provide for us. It can provide guidance and is an extension of the family. That same community watches over all of us and makes us safer. The community has our back. Years ago, this was literally true. Neighbors next door would tell you if someone suspicious was hanging around your house. If you got into mischief, the neighbors would chastise you. People in a community look out for one another.

In ancient African society, community meant even more. There was a social bond that required that those who had more helped those with less. A stranger or poor person was treated with respect and welcomed into homes. In these communities, women and men shared power and responsibility.

Long ago in the US slave communities, under horrible conditions of oppression, the slaves managed to survive. This was despite the fact they were often treated no better than farm animals. They survived over two hundred years because of community. They took care of one another as well as each other's children. They shared the scraps they had and, through nothing less than a miracle, managed a few moments of song and worship on Sundays.

Our sense of community strengthens us. Community is not a place you leave easily. It is a place where you grow and live. It is where your roots are. It is where people love and care for us. Often children or teenagers are focused on getting away from home. But there is something wrong with the notion that our lives would somehow be better away for those who love us, those who nurture us.

You can make the biggest difference in your life and the lives of others by working to improve your community. It's not a matter of just giving back. It is staying engaged every day. Your community can thrive if everyone sees it as a potential oasis. It takes your time and effort to realize that potential.

Emotional State

Your emotional state has a lot to do with your happiness. How you feel about yourself affects how you see the world and how you fit into that world. If you feel that you are not worthy—not worth anything—you may think any and everyone is better than you. If you are hopeless, you will feel you have nothing to look forward to, no plan for your life. If your attitude is poor, your view of the world will be negative and your motivation low. Here are three areas where you can work to improve your happiness.

Self-Worth

Happiness is knowing you are worthy and that you have value. It does not refer to how much money you have. It is internal. Everyone has value, but not everyone appreciates their own value. Developing a sense of self-worth requires work. It begins with setting goals for yourself and then working to achieve them. Each goal achieved will enhance your confidence. If you do not give yourself continual challenges, you'll feel as though you are falling behind.

Your goal is not to beat out someone else, but to establish your own to-do list. After all, this is about you and your dream. If you make it about proving you are better than someone else, you'll eventually lose your focus. Competition is a fine thing in moderation. My perspective on life is that you can live your life to the fullest without leaving a trail of losers behind you.

If life is only about winners, what does that leave for the rest of us? If losing is a necessary evil, who picks the losers? Where is the landfill where the losers live? It is truly terrible that some people believe that they were born losers. Apparently, those around them did not have the wherewithal to explain the truth to them. As long as your focus is shortsighted, your imagination limited, and your motivation low, you will accept a loser diagnosis.

Everyone has something he or she does well. You've got to figure out what this is for you and nurture it. This is far more constructive than taking someone else's strength and transplanting that onto you. Your body will reject this transplant, and you'll feel worse than when you started. Find your own strength, and grow it.

Don't compare your weaknesses to someone else's strengths. Compare, if need be, strengths with strengths. Preferably, just work to be your best.

Hope

Hope is a seed, and happiness is the plant that grows from that seed. Hope is the feeling that you can achieve your goals. It works hand in hand with desire, driving us to reach our potential. Hope is motivating; it is the reason you and I get up in the morning. It is the reason you couldn't wait to grow up when you were little. Hope feeds our dreams. The greater the hope, the bigger the dream.

You deserve your best possible future. The fuel that powers your dreams is hope. Believe in yourself. Believe that you deserve a phenomenal future. As an important leader once said, you must always work to "keep hope alive." What this means is that there will be setbacks, no matter how well you plan. But you must keep pursuing your dream. Some setbacks can turn your world upside down, like a death of a family member or your parents getting divorced. Sometimes just moving to a different house can hurt, because you have to leave your friends.

One way "to keep hope alive" is to learn how to grieve. Grieving is how you deal with hurt. It is important to learn to grieve so that you can release your emotions and come to peace with your feelings of loss and hurt. If you do not release these bad feelings through the grieving process, the pain will take over your life. You might act out these bad feelings, hurting yourself and others. If you need help dealing with grief talk to your parents about getting medical help. It will change your life in a wonderful way.

Attitude

Your attitude can be positive, negative, or in-between. It reflects how you feel about your life. Do you see challenges you can conquer, or do you see problems that are piling up like traffic on a freeway at rush hour. Perhaps you just don't care about your life or about anyone else. When you don't care, it's called apathy. This is the worst attitude to have, because you are stuck doing nothing as everyone else moves on with their lives. People with apathy have no purpose, goals, hope, or feelings of self-worth. They are just empty shells. Apathy is not a healthy attitude.

The best part about attitude is that, with knowledge and experience, your attitude can change—and usually it improves. The more you know and understand, the more able you are to see answers to life's problems. You dream, hope, and feel confident about yourself because you feel in control.

So, the key to positive attitude change is your thirst for information. Listen to those who know, such as your parents and teachers. Ask questions about life, school subjects, and options for your future. Ask these questions of people who have earned your respect and trust. Once you've asked your question, listen and learn. Don't waste your valuable time listening to useless chatter about things that will not improve your life.

As you begin to find answers to your questions, you will come up with more questions, and this is okay. There is a lot to learn in life. The more you understand, the more confident you will be and the more enlightened your attitude will become. A positive attitude will empower you to become the Most Valuable Player, the star in your life.

Change your attitude the easy way by finding reasons to smile. Begin and end each day with a smile. Sprinkle smiles throughout your day. You will feel happier, and others will feel better about you. It's free and so simple. There's nothing to lose, and a whole boatload of happiness to gain. Smile often.

Work on keeping your attitude productive. Feed your dreams and hopes with information as if it were ice cream—but in this case the result will be sweet satisfaction. Keep your emotional state positive, and you will find that there are many good choices you can make. With good choices, your feeling of self-worth will grow and grow.

Money and Possessions

In the 1960s, the Beatles became one of the most famous rock groups of all time. They had many hit songs, one of which was "Can't Buy Me Love." A part of the song goes like this: "I may not have a lot to give but what I got I'll give to you. I don't care too much for money, money can't buy me love."

Money and possessions matter, but beware. Like a kid with a bulging stomach and chocolate all over his face, you may be smiling now, but just wait. Too much of a good thing can make you sick. Pursuing only money and possessions, can be like candy to a little kid. As you grow and learn, you will better understand money's cause and effect.

No one wants to merely survive. You want to thrive. So becoming rich is a noble goal, right? Actually, happiness should be your goal. Money plays a part, but if you make it more important than your family or friends, you are missing the point. If you think that all you have to offer someone is your money, you are still missing the point. The point is what the Beatles said, "Money can't buy me love." It won't buy you love either.

Your true value is the love you share. It is about giving of yourself more than giving of your things. When a loved one or friend moves away, you are sad. For most of us, it is because we honestly miss having that person around, spending time with us, sharing, and caring.

We can become confused and overvalue money. If you close your eyes and think about the best movements in your life, how many of them were about money? Maybe on Christmas or your birthday you got a fantastic present. But were you all alone or were you with family and friends? How would you have felt if you got a fabulous present and there were no family or friends to share your excitement? I think you'd feel sad, lonely, and hurt. So, if money and possessions were the answer to a happy life, money and presents would be enough. They are not.

List five key points you want to remember from this chapter:

1.

2.

3.

4.

5.

Projects

1. List several things that you do well.

2. List several things that you are passionate about.

3. List several areas you would like to learn more about, and get started learning that information.

4. Watch the Beatles video "Can't Buy Me Love" on YouTube

Suggested Reading

Hispanic-American Scientists by Walter Olesky

Chapter 5

WHAT IS SUCCESS?

Profile: Jeremy Sicile-Kira

About Jeremy

Success is relative. That means that you and I measure success by our own rules. Success is not only about money and fame, it's also about love. It is a reflection of how you treat and care for yourself and others. You must work for and earn your victories. Here is Jeremy's story. Read it, and you'll see what I mean.

Jeremy Sicile-Kira was born in France in 1989. He now lives in California with his family. His dad, Daniel, is a design consultant and construction project manager. Jeremy's mom, Chantal, has a bachelor's degree in social ecology and has worked as a teacher, therapist, blogger, and radio show host. Today she is best known as an award-winning writer.

Jeremy was very fortunate to be born into a loving family where both parents have worked tirelessly to help him enjoy a wonderful life. Sometime after his birth, Jeremy's parents notice that he did not seem to be responsive when they played with him. They took him to doctors to find out why he acted as he did, and at the age of three he was diagnosed as severely autistic. This meant that Jeremy had a mental disorder that made it hard for him to interact with other people. In addition, a person with autism may also not behave well in certain situations and continuously repeat the same movements or gestures.

Jeremy's diagnosis was made even more heartbreaking when doctor's explained that he would not even be able to speak. His parents encouraged him to do his best year after year. His mom homeschooled him without knowing if he understood what she was saying.

When Jeremy was fifteen, his mom started to use a letter board to help him communicate. He would point at letters to spell words, which his mother would read. It turned out that Jeremy understood everything that was being said to him. He had waited years, trapped in his own body, to talk to his family. This breakthrough, with the letter board, changed everything.

Over time, Jeremy enrolled at Torrey Pines High School in California. He attended mostly special education classes but also was allowed to take some general courses with the other students. In 2010 Jeremy completed all his course requirements for graduation with a B+ grade point average. He is the first nonverbal autistic student to graduate from Torrey Pines High. Jeremy was selected to give a speech at the graduation ceremony, which he did with computer voice-assisted software on his laptop.

Jeremy worked and succeeded under very tough conditions, and he still has to struggle with it every day. The joy, happiness, and prosperity he has experienced his entire life was not just due to his hard work; his family's love and devotion played a big part as well.

Status

Status is the material side of success. If you achieve status as a result of how others perceive you, it could have a positive effect. If you chase after status like a dog after a cat, someone is going to get hurt. It is likely that that someone will be you or someone you care about. Status, like a new day, happens. It's not a worthy goal in and of itself.

All of us look up to someone who appears to have an enviable life. And it's absolutely necessary for us to set goals for ourselves. Set your goals and make them big! But don't confuse the appetizer with the main course. It's not about the bling; it's about a dream life of love and happiness. You can achieve your goals and have a great life without becoming a zillionaire, but if you do become a zillionaire, pay attention to what is important. Embracing life and making the world a better place is important.

Status is the material side and result of success. Aim high and let status happen.

Who Do You Admire?

It's easy to admire people because of their status: their bling and other physical signs of comfort, power, and fun. So sports, music, and movie stars may top your list of people you admire. It is more appropriate to include your parents, teachers, even a few of your friends. You admire them because of their real and positive impact on your life. Because they care about you. Because they are good and kind.

So, on the one hand, there are people you don't really know, and yet you choose to idolize them. You buy shoes or sport drinks because they recommend these products. They make money off you and share nothing with you. Your friends at school may let you borrow their belongings. They might even share half of their lunch just to be nice.

Why do you and I admire the stranger who only wants our money more than someone who cares for us? It sounds backward. You should reserve your devotion for those who have earned it.

So, my definition of a successful person is one who is a role model to others. There are some stars who meet this test. No one is perfect, but all of our actions matter. A famous singer who beats his spouse does not warrant admiration. He needs help. A fabulously rich movie starlet who only cares about herself may not warrant our admiration. She may need our empathy.

On the other hand, learn about your would-be idols. Find out what you can about them, especially their conduct. With the total picture, decide if you still admire them. Parents, teachers, and friends consistently pass the admiration test. Typically you see much more acceptable conduct in those who care for you. That's why you admire them.

Money and More Things

What matters most about money is what you do with it. Money is not "the root of all evil." You determine if it is used for good or bad. In a country overflowing with wealth like the United States, why is there so much poverty, homelessness, and hopelessness? Are the people suffering from these problems unable to manage their money well, or is there something else at play?

From the day you saw your first internet or TV advertisement, you received one of your first lessons on selfishness. Businesses spend a lot of money to make us believe their products are fun and exciting. Guess what? It works! From smartphones to soda and makeup to munchies, we love it. It's sort of like a Disney Pixar movie, great fun, but it's fantasy. It's thrilling while we are in the moment, an escape from our humdrum lives. And escape is something we need to do every now and then to keep our sanity. Yes, escape can be healthy. So my message to you is it is important to have balance in your life. Money can help you with that balance whether you use it for escape or charity. Like the fun movie keep your perspective about how you use money.

Pace yourself and work, not wish, for improvement in your economic situation. A rule of physics, Sir Isaac Newton's First Law of Motion, is that an object in motion tends to stay in motion and an object at rest tends to stay at rest. Be an object in motion. Do constructive things to help your family. It's okay to collect nice things, but don't let their importance outweigh the importance of your family or your moral values. Your life will go on just fine if you don't get every new thing. Buy the *next* new thing or the one after that. Possessions only matter for the moment. Do you remember all the toys you, as a kid, thought you could not do without? You survived just fine. Don't get caught in the pursuit of the next shiny thing; it could well harm you or your family for a lifetime.

When you assess your wealth, don't just count the dollars. *Count your family, your positive relationships, your future opportunities, and your motivation to improve yourself.* Count your blessings.

Be a Phoenix

In ancient Egypt, the phoenix symbolized long life and renewal. The story goes that this ancient bird, which looked similar to an eagle, had a lifespan over five hundred years. At the end of its life, it would fly to the ancient Egyptian city of Lunu (the Greeks call it Heliopolis). *Lunu* means "pillar," which according to mythology was the place where all creation began.

But back to our story. The phoenix would make a nest somewhere in Luna. There, after laying an egg, the bird would die in a blaze of flames. From this fire would rise a new or reborn mighty phoenix. In this way it cheated death and lived on in immortality.

American is to people what Lunu was to the phoenix. Immigrants come here to start their lives anew. Citizens of this wonderful country have the opportunity to be born again at any time. This is not just a religious or spiritual second chance but a moral, educational, and career reboot. You can go down in a whimper or a blaze. With focus, hard work, and good will, any of us can make ourselves vibrant again.

Like the phoenix, you can rise up from the flames in a blaze of triumph and glory. You can be that shining light that helps others find their way. You can rise from the ashes of a poor neighborhood or a troubled family. Like the phoenix, you can breathe new life into this world, your neighborhood, and your family. Success is when you find your way and go back to help the rest of us.

Your triumph, like the phoenix will live on and on. Your love for others, family, and those you meet only in passing is the truest measure of accomplishment. You have the opportunity to live forever in the hearts of others. You should take advantage of this gift of renewal.

List five key points you want to remember from this chapter:

1.

2.

3.

4.

5.

Projects

1. List several areas where you are rich, and explain why (family, friends, etc.).

2. List several areas where you are poor, and explain why.

3. List five ways you can share the things that make you rich.

4. List five ways you can increase the things that make your life rich.

5. List commercials and advertisements of items you like. What kind of people are in the commercial? Are they having a great time, especially while they are using the product? Have you used the product, and do you feel like the people in the commercial?

Suggested Reading

- www.jeremysicilekira.com

- www.chantalsicile-kira.com

- http://www.mtv.com/videos/true-life-i-have-autism/1554937/playlist.jhtml

- *Tony Hawk: Professional Skateboarder by Tony* Hawk

Chapter 6

TOOLS YOU MUST HAVE

Profile: Sukyana Roy

About Sukyana

What tools do you need to succeed and have a happy life? Well, it will come as no surprise that you already know all the tools I will be reviewing. In this chapter you will gain a better understanding of why these should be important to you.

It is true that the "best things in life are free," but you have been trained to think that the more something costs, the better it is. That is true for diamonds and gold, but there are things more precious. A family's love or the support of a close friend is free and yet priceless at the same time. You expect your family and friends to take care of you, without pay, because they love you. So is their love important? You bet it is!

With that perspective, let's take a look at Sukyana Roy. She has taken the nurturing support of her family and several of the tools in this chapter—including school, personal goals, and patience—and combined them with hard work to win international recognition. Like her, you can find your passion and get to work. Here's Sukyana's story.

Sukyana Roy was raised in the middle-class Philadelphia suburb of Montgomery County. Her parents are originally from India. She placed in the top twenty in the Scripps Spelling Bee Championships two years in a row. In 2011 she won this event. She proved to be the best though thousands of schools and perhaps hundreds of thousands of students participated in the fifty states, the District of Columbia, American Samoa, Guam, Puerto Rico, US Virgin Islands, and Department of Defense Dependents Schools in Europe—as well as the Bahamas, Canada, China, Ghana, Jamaica, Japan, New Zealand, and South Korea.

There are only 275 regional champions who make it to the international semifinal championship. After several rounds of competition, only forty-five finalists are left. As an eighth-grader Sukyana won first place over the runner-up from Canada. But, more importantly, she achieved international acclaim at age 14! Way to make the rest of us feel like under achievers.

Sukyana is active in school, obviously loves words, and wants to travel and have a career in international relations. She is smart, but as with all high achievers, she works very hard. With the support of her parents, she has weathered the enormous stress of international competition and come through with flying colors.

In preparation for the 2011 Scripps Championship, she actually studied an unabridged dictionary word by word, page by page, not once but twice. She won the bee after completing over twenty-one grueling rounds. Her winning word was *cymotrichous*.

Who would have guessed that by being an excellent speller you could win over 40,000 dollars, get featured on ESPN in primetime, and become a celebrity? Being a proficient speller can pay off—really.

School

School is essential because it is your key to prosperity. Its sole purpose is to open the door to your future. It is your best chance to become all that you can be.

School is the greatest, most important gift your government can give you. It's where you learn the power of reading, science, numbers, and the arts. The whole world is made available to you. Through books, videos, people of all occupations, and field trips, you are immersed in the marvels of this world. School is a blessing in many ways.

School was your first opportunity to learn social skills (beginning in daycare and preschool). You learned how to treat others; you learned what behavior is acceptable and what is not.

School is a treasure chest of basic knowledge and eye-opening experiences. As you progress through the grades, you climb another step on your way to the mountaintop of self-fulfillment. As you climb that scary, yet exciting mountain, you have to learn as you go. You have to adapt to surprises. You can complete this trek only by calling on the basic skills you have learned. It may be necessary to put several fundamental pieces of knowledge together in a unique way to conquer a new problem. This is called creative thought or ingenuity. This is a type of knowledge you get in school.

Believe it or not, you will remember at least one of your elementary teachers for the rest of your life. This is because elementary school is one of your most positive learning experiences. You have the same teacher for most of your subjects. That teacher knows you well, what you do best, and where you need help. That teacher also gives you a lot of attention and support.

The closer relationship you have with your teachers in elementary school is key to your learning. Elementary school is the best time to work on basics. If for some reason you still need work on basic reading, writing, and math, have no fear. With help you can solve this setback. The sooner you get going the better. Even if you are in middle or high school it is not too late. Work with your teachers and counselors for possible options. Tutors, mentors, and hard work can get you back on track if you need to catch up.

Library

Before there was the Internet, there was the library. Before Google and Yahoo, there was the card catalog. Before Facebook, there were biographies. Libraries have existed since ancient times, even before the Romans or Greeks. You could argue that ancient writings on cave walls were the first libraries— each series of drawings, a book. We humans have always had the need to share our story. Our great thinkers documented their achievements to share with posterity.

Today libraries are more important than ever. In many ways, a library is easier to navigate than the Internet. Libraries come with expert guides called librarians. The beauty of a library is its wealth of detailed information. In a library you are surrounded by the world's best minds and not just someone doing casual blogging.

Certainly I am not trying to pick a fight with hardcore Internet users. My point is that there are many places to get information.

It's not an issue of some being outdated and others being newer or better. You can learn a lot from the Internet, books, videos, and especially other people. But the minute you isolate yourself to one source of information, you limit your perspective.

Use your school library and those in your community. Take the time to wander through and look at all there is to see. Think of it as an interactive trip to a museum of books, DVDs, and CDs. You can also find e-books and audio books, so there is no reason you cannot experience the wonder of books. A challenging book can not only teach you something new, it can also change your outlook on life. It can take you to times past and future, to other countries, into space, or into the worlds of fantasy and science fiction. Books release our imagination in a way no other medium does.

Go to your school or local library, and find a book that interests you. It really should be something you want to read. It can be serious or silly. All that matters is that it is something that grabs your interest. If you find the right book, you'll make many more trips to your library. It will become an enjoyable adventure that lasts a lifetime.

Museums

Close to libraries in importance are museums. A museum is a time machine filled with the wonders of the past. It is especially exciting when you can touch items. But just the same, it's a neat opportunity for time travel. You can venture back to the early days of America and see the homes, clothes, and tools. You can go back to the early days of knights, kings, and queens in medieval times. You can get an idea of how early Native Americans lived.

If you're lucky, you can see a real mummy or a dinosaur skeleton. Just think about it: at a museum you may be able to see a person from three thousand years ago or a dinosaur from 200 million years ago. That's incredible to even imagine. What a treasure to be able to walk back in time, gain some understanding of where you came from, and how your ancestors and the world have evolved! Museums are precious family photo albums of all the creatures, plants, and mysterious forces that gave birth to our world today.

Go to a museum any time you can. Every time will be different. Every time will be a fun chance to learn.

Internet

The Internet opens up a world of information. You probably spend much of your time just being entertained by all the interesting text, pictures, and videos. You can play video games with your neighbors. You can blog or tweet or post on Facebook.

What was once a tool of scientific research is today quite different. The Internet has so much untapped potential. Think about what it would be like to have a Facebook friend in France who could help you learn to speak French. How about having the opportunity to work on a science project with a Russian or Chinese student? Stuff like this is already happening. People often work together writing songs and books on the Internet.

There is so much more. Just dream it—and do it. Like any other medium, it is defined by the user. Think big. It is not just a smartphone or television replacement.

Today most Americans have access to the Internet in their homes or through their libraries, YMCAs, and so on. Take the time to get good at using it. Because it can be used by anyone, there is a lot of good—and bad—information that can be easily accessed. Have fun, be careful, but move forward. Use it to improve your life, to find answers, and to better understand the choices you have available to you. It is a tool that you must master if you expect to realize your best life.

Patience

Patience is a valuable tool. Without a healthy dose of patience, life can be extremely frustrating and unsatisfying. Your family and relationships will suffer. Your ability to be compassionate and to empathize will be limited.

Patience is a discipline that must be learned and practiced early in life. Deep breathing exercises, regular exercise, and even meditation can help you with your patience. Work on this. Don't be afraid to engage in tasks that require your attention for an extended period. This will improve your relationships and your ability to accomplish your goals. Random wandering does not help you achieve; purposeful actions do.

Patience can also improve your ability to listen. Instead of blurting out every thought that crosses your mind, stop and let the other person finish speaking. Your friends and others who know you will be impressed when you are able to master this skill. When you stop to listen to others, you'll have a better understanding of their perspective. They will want to talk to you because you listen. Another way you can do to help your listening skill is to concentrate on what the other person is saying. When they're finished, repeat in your own words what you thought they said. Do this in personal conversations, but not when your teacher is speaking to the whole class.

Lots of teens participate in sports. It's exciting and fun. It is also a great investment in patience and training. By high school young athletes can spend 10-20 hours a week in training, practice sessions, and events. Whether or not you are even a starter, many of you are happy to make the sacrifice to belong, to win. But what about after your time for playing sports is over? Even the pro's have to plan for life after sports. Many of them also invested their time in studying science, math, language, and the arts. Patience helps them and you to win the game. It helps you to understand your role with the team. More importantly, patience, helps you win in life. It also allows us to pursue more than one long term goal simultaneously. Patience can make a huge difference in your future success. You can reap a lifetime of benefits by learning to exercise patience.

Safe Haven

It is important to have a safe place. This is somewhere you can go to study, think, and play—a place free of violence. A place where there are responsible adults who look out for you. Sometimes this is not at your school or even in your neighborhood. You may have an aunt or grandparent to spend time with or a church or community center with security. The YMCA or Boys and Girls Club are excellent choices. Find the right place for you, get your parent's approval, and go there when you don't feel safe otherwise.

If you do not feel safe, you won't be at your best. Fear, worry, and anxiety will drive your actions. You will not be able to concentrate on positive things like your education. Your only goal may be survival. You are not an animal in the wild; you are a thinking, caring person. You have much to offer this world. Don't let bad circumstances cage you in to a life of despair.

I cannot stress this enough. The world can be dangerous. If you ignore cause and effect and get hurt, it may not be a mere accident. A dangerous environment can produce bad results. Your outcome does not have to be bad if you life in a dangerous neighborhood. This is a fact. Take care of yourself and those you love. Look out for your safety.

List five key points you want to remember from this chapter:

1.

2.

3.

4.

5.

Projects

1. At least every two weeks, visit your local or school library.

2. Visit local museums with family and friends, and after every visit, write down what you enjoyed most.

3. Write a list of at least five goals. Review these goals every few months to see if you are making progress toward achieving them.

4. Develop a list of safe havens, including names and phone numbers of people to contact when you need help.

Suggested Reading

Gifted Hands: The Ben Carson Story (Kid's Edition) by Greg Lewis

Chapter 7

LEARNING TO EXCEL

Profile: Angela Zhang

About Angela

Learning to excel may seem like something that comes naturally, something that you are born with. But like so many important skills, it is something you have to learn. It involves learning about yourself, what excites or motivates you. It's about what you are capable of, and what you'd like to do most of all with your life. If you can find the answer to these questions, you'll be well on the way to finding your place, your purpose in life.

You don't want to underestimate yourself. Later in life you don't want to wonder, *What if I had tried this or that?* Like Angela Zhang, you can find your passion. You can find it early in your life and start travelling down that road toward your best future. Once you understand what you are capable of, no one will have to push you to fulfill your potential. You will take the opportunity and run, just like Angela. Here's her story.

Angela Zhang lives in the upper-middle-class Silicon Valley hub of Cupertino. Her hometown is also the location of the Apple, like in iPhone, headquarters. Of Cupertino's 54,000 residents, over 60 percent have at least a bachelor's degree, and 40 percent were born outside the United States. In fact, both of Angela's parents are Chinese immigrants.

So, what's so special about Angela? Well as a seventeen-year-old student at Monta Vista High, she distinguished herself by writing a research paper concerning a cure for cancer. She has been interested in bioengineering since her freshman year, when she began to read doctorate-level research. In her sophomore year, she found an opportunity to work at a lab at Stanford University. A year later, while still a high school student, she was performing her own research in that lab.

CBS newsman Steve Hartman explained Angela's work: "Angela's idea was to mix cancer medicine in a polymer that would attach to nanoparticles—nanoparticles that would then attach to cancer cells and show up on an MRI so doctors could see exactly where the tumors are. Then she thought that if you aimed an infrared light at the tumors to melt the polymer and release the medicine, thus killing the cancer cells while leaving healthy cells completely unharmed." Okay, I don't know about you, but I think that's awesome and complicated. Angela also entered her research project in the Siemens Science Contest; she won first place and 100,000 dollars.

Angela works hard in school, and her favorite subjects are any and all of the sciences. Her can-do attitude has a lot to do with her curiosity, drive, and ability to dream big. But even with a brilliant scientific mind, she still finds time to enjoy shopping and buying a nice pair of shoes. Let it be known that excellent students have fun too.

Your Brain

In learning to excel, our first stop is the human brain. The human brain may be the most magnificent organism in existence. Just look at all the things the human mind has conceived. Wow! Our brain is so complex that there is still a great deal scientists do not yet know about it. For example, regardless of what you see on cartoons, scientists don't know why a bigger brain is not necessarily a smarter brain. And how do you explain people who are autistic savants? These individual's minds can perform highly specialized and advanced functions in specific areas. At the same time, they are developmentally challenged and may not be able to interact socially with their peers. For example, they may be able to play complex music on a piano, note for note, after hearing the song only once. Others can solve extremely difficult math equations in their head without pencil or paper.

All that you are and all that you can be is locked away in your brain, just waiting to be released. Every beat of your heart and every breath you take is controlled by your brain. Have you ever wondered what causes you to wake up every day? There are so many things within us that we take for granted. We just assume our bodies will function and life will go on, because it happens without thought. Oh, but there is thought in every motion you make. There are millions of electrochemical (part electrical energy and part chemical energy) interactions happening in our brain even in our sleep. These actions keep our body functioning and maturing. Your brain not only helps you in mental actions, it helps in physical activities as well. The coordination of your arms, legs, and eyes when you catch a football, swim, kick a soccer ball, or play Ping-Pong depends on signals from your brain to other parts of your body. This is why an injury to your head can cause so much harm.

Your brain is also where you feel love (not really your heart); it controls your mood—happy or sad or in between. It can be said that your soul resides in your brain—all of your potential for good and bad—also known as your conscience. I am not going to cover how your brain accomplishes all that it does; that would take quoting lots of thick and complicated books. What is important for now is that you have an idea of some of the things your brain does.

Don't take your brain for granted; feed it with information, positive thoughts, and healthy food. If your brain is healthy, generally speaking, you will be happy, hopeful, motivated, productive, and understanding of other people. Protect your brain; it controls your future.

Types of Learners

There are many types of learners. The three main categories are those who learn best by listening, seeing, or touching/experiencing. People who learn mostly by listening tend to discuss things and get input before moving ahead. Seeing is visual learning. These people like to read and web browse to get background information. People who learn well from touch and experience like physically working through a problem. You will find all three styles in each chapter of this book.

This is an exciting time in education. Teachers, psychologist and other professionals have a greater understanding of how individuals learn. They also have a better idea of how different social, medical, and economic conditions impact a student's ability to learn. In the old days if you had difficulty learning the options were limited. Now you need to make sure your parents and teachers know exactly where you are having problems. Don't worry about being ashamed or scared. Get help. You don't have to struggle all alone. The answers to your problem may take time or it may be solved as easily as asking the right question.

In order for you to do your best, there has to be a three-way communication link that includes you, your parents, and your teacher. Each link is responsible to the other two. Each is important; like a stool, if you lose one of the legs, you will be in an unstable situation. Each person in the link has to be involved with both strong points and weaknesses in your education. There may be a need to focus more on a specific learning method at home and at school. There may also be a need to bring in another person, such as a tutor, special education teacher, reading specialist, or even a medical specialist, to find out if there is a biological issue that is impacting your ability to learn.

Understanding your learning type is just the beginning to becoming a high achiever in school. Constant communication is one of the best ways to identify your learning type and to succeed. Apply principle five from chapter one, "Life Is a Team Sport." Communicate with your team: your parents and teacher. The result of great team work is that you will become a winner in life.

Your Potential

So, who is to say what you are capable or not capable of learning? I think your potential is unlimited. Teaching methods matter as does, a student's readiness to learn, and the use of technology. With all the right tools in place, anyone can excel. I'm not just talking about a basic understanding, I mean mastery. Why can't you make all A's in elementary school? Why can't you keep getting them in middle and high school? As breakthroughs are made in our understanding of the brain, how learning takes place, and the effects of nutrition and emotional state, there are reasons to be hopeful. Today all students who work hard can set the bar high. They can work with their support team of, teachers, parents, tutors, mentors, and technologist to produce the breakthrough needed to achieve their goal.

Today technology offers more opportunities in how education is provided. One example of the technology breakthroughs in education is the Kahn Academy, www.kahnacademy.org. This is a free, online education system. The academy offers interactive lessons that are detailed and short. If you are struggling with math or science or other subjects, you can find your area of interest and take an easy-to-understand module. This training system also includes a means for teachers, parents, and mentors to monitor student progress. This system frees the teacher from spending most of their time in front of the class and allows them to concentrate their valuable time with individual students who need their help.

The real benefit of Kahn Academy is that each student goes at his or her own pace. You're not finished with a subject until you have mastered it, independent of the rest of the class. It also encourages student initiative and lets every student go as fast as he or she can in any subject area. Consider that one of our greatest minds in physics, Albert Einstein, struggled in school because he disliked the rigid methods of his teachers. Kahn Academy may not be the final answer in education but it is one example of how we can apply technology to improve learning.

Your education should be one of your top priorities. Dream big and look at limits as temporary and not permanent. Who's to say if you can be the next great artist, teacher, architect or business mogul? So, starting now, work to prepare yourself for your best future.

Quick Self-Evaluation

How are you doing in school? Do your grades indicate that you are weak in certain subjects? Do you know why you score lower in certain subjects? Have you worked with your teacher, parents, and friends, and have you tried a tutor? Maybe you have just accepted your grades—good, average, or bad–as the way it will be. You may think there's nothing wrong and nothing that should be changed. Things are okay and your performance is about the same as your peers. Garbage! School, especially elementary school, isn't brain surgery. In sports, when you are not proficient at something, the coach makes you practice that skill until you get it right. If you can spend three hours practicing jump shots or your volleyball serve, why can't you also devote that time to math, language arts, or science? Why is extra coaching a normal part of sports but not normal in the subjects that will determine your future? What's up with that?!

So, part of the problem with low grades is the standard you set for yourself. Raise your standards, because you can do better. Remember, low standards equal low grades.

The next part of your self-evaluation is understanding how you learn. Do you know what kind of teaching method and study method works best for you? Do you perform better in groups or alone? Do you remember more when you are able to touch and feel something? Do you need to see how a topic applies to you? Do you learn faster by reading or by interacting with a computer, video, and sound? Understand what works best for you, and use it to improve your grades and performance in school.

Remember to apply yourself. Learning can be fun, but it is also a lot of work. The more you succeed, the more you will enjoy learning. You don't have to be average, and you don't have to settle. What you have to do is understand how you learn and work to excel. Don't sell yourself short. Gather all your tools and support group, use your best learning method, and go for it.

The Importance of Questioning

You learn by questioning and doing. If you don't ask questions, everyone assumes you understand the subject. The opposite could be true: your lack of questions could mean that you don't understand the material. Get accustomed to asking questions. There may be several ways of looking at a problem and more than one way to solve it. Test yourself by asking questions, such as restating what you thought you heard your teacher say as a question. Remember what I said about patience and developing your listening skills? Apply that here. You'll be surprised that at times what you heard was not what the teacher meant. Had you not raised a question, you might have remained confused.

You may feel that people who ask questions don't seem smart. Perhaps you feel embarrassed about asking a question in front of the whole class. Don't worry. Smart students always ask questions. Anyone who is good at their job asks a lot of questions as well. People who ask questions care enough to get things right. They pay attention to details. You wouldn't want a doctor to operate on your heart and in the middle of the surgery whisper to the nurse, "I really wish I had asked about this type of heart surgery when I was an intern."

Questions have spurred humankind's greatest discoveries. Ask.

List five key points you want to remember from this chapter:

1.

2.

3.

4.

5.

Projects

1. Go to the Kahn Academy website, www.khanacademy.org, and look for a topic that you have had problems with in school. Take the lesson, and see if it makes a difference. If it's in any way better for you, include Kahn in your normal study routine.

2. Identify learning opportunities outside of school.

3. Determine what types of learning works best for you. Discuss this with your parents.

4. Identify people you can turn to for help, such as tutors.

Suggested Reading

100 African-Americans Who Shaped American History by Chrisanne Becker

Chapter 8

INVESTING IN YOU

Profile: Umar Brimah

About Umar

Some people live like there is no tomorrow. They don't plan, save, or try to learn more. They just live for fun today. As you study history, you will find that no successful American lived that way. The people who make history dream, plan, work, and save. They work for a better tomorrow and to be the best person they can be.

Achieving a big goal takes time. A period of preparation has to take place. There is a time of trial and error that is a valuable learning and growing experience.

Umar Brimah is a young man with hopes and dreams. He has many interests, including science and business. He is investing his time in pursuing those interests, and he is learning from his many experiences. Umar is preparing himself–in a big way–for the future. He has support from his mom as well as from friends who share his passions. He is just one of many young people who has the courage to step up and take a chance on a dream.

You can step up as well. Whatever your dreams and passions, you can get started now to prepare the way to your best life. You can be Umar in your own way. There's nothing to lose but your fear, so start today investing in yourself. Here is Umar Brimah's story.

Cape Girardeau, Missouri, is a working-class city of about 35,000 residents. It is in the southeast section of the state and about 115 miles from St. Louis. Until 2008 the city was known primarily for Southeast Missouri State University. Now, thanks to Umar Brimah, it is also known as the town that has a twelve-year-old chief executive officer of a business. Umar's favorite hobby is collecting anime–Japanese cartoon characters. He came up with the idea to open a store in Girardeau, because he believed that other collectors were tired of paying double the price for anime collectables on the Internet. His mom loaned him ten thousand dollars of seed money to purchase a shop on Broadway Street and buy his initial inventory.

So his store, Yumazu, was born. (That's his name in Japanese.) So far, his business is showing a profit. Umar's mom hopes that he will be able to raise enough money to pay for his college education. Besides being a business owner, Umar also has an interest in science and engineering. He is a member of the Ironman Robotics team. The team is made up of twelve students from various towns in Southeast Missouri who participate in a statewide science competition. Umar's group placed first in a state contest and third in the regionals. Who knows, with his interests in engineering and anime, perhaps one day he will develop a superhero crime fighting robot. Dreams, hard work, and family support are a powerful combination.

Tomorrow Will Come

Tomorrow will come. Just as you expect to wake up in the morning, tomorrow will come. So, how do you take advantage of this sure bet? You have an obligation to make tomorrow better than today. Even if you are satisfied with where you are, you still have to plan for what comes next. Remember Newton's First Law of Motion: an object in motion tends to stay in motion? Likewise, an object at rest tends to stay at rest. Make staying in motion your motto. Unless you get up and start moving, you're not going anywhere.

Tomorrow will come. You've got to get in motion, or life will pass you by. You've got nothing to lose and the whole world to gain. Any step forward is progress. Whether you are taking tiny steps or giant leaps, progress is progress. You should strive for a fabulous life—one that highlights taking chances, excitement and fulfillment.

Tomorrow will come. Challenge yourself to be your best. Education is the most powerful investment you can make to achieve your dreams. Following your dreams can be the carrot that motivates you to go on and on and on. Establish goals and work to achieve those goals, even if you're only making tiny steps every day. Progress is progress.

Tomorrow will come.

Time for Me

Call it quiet time. Call it alone time. But you don't have to be alone or in a quiet space. What is important is that your mind is at peace. You can get there by listening to music, reading a book, or doing yoga. Just make sure you give yourself time to recharge, to take a deep breath, to hang your worries like a big coat on a hook.

Time for *you* is important. It is not at all selfish; it is preservation. It is how you prepare to face this tough world with renewed vigor and positive feelings. You can't give your best to yourself or others if you are worn down. You will not be alert for those once-in-a-lifetime opportunities or have the confidence to walk away from bad choices unless your mind is clear.

So find time for yourself. Drive and hard work are necessary, but working too much can cause more harm than good. Push, recuperate, and push again. Your body and mind can deal with stress more efficiently after periods of rest. As with many things in life and nature, there is a balance that we must maintain.

Pay attention to your body signals. Do you lack energy or interest in things that you normally like? Are you always sleepy or distracted? Do you have problems concentrating? Do you always seem to be getting sick lately? All of these can be signs of stress or overwork. When your body gives you these signs, stop and pay attention. Take the time to figure out what is wrong, and get help. Like most problems, stress can get worse over time. Work to always be at your best. That includes taking time for yourself.

Good Health

Engaging in regular exercise and healthy habits improves your mind. It helps your concentration and ability to work through problems. It also improves your mood through the release of certain chemicals in your brain which, among other things, give you a sense of well-being. Your health can make the difference between a positive and energetic attitude and a helpless state of mind.

Exercise can be aerobic, like running, or anaerobic, like weightlifting or push-ups. You need to do both. The aerobic exercise will improve your blood flow and strengthen your heart and lungs. Anaerobic exercise will strengthen your muscles, making it easier for you to lift things, improving your posture, and improving your metabolism—your ability to burn fat.

Next, as much as possible, eat healthy. Unhealthy eating can lead to all sorts of illnesses, such as high blood pressure and diabetes, which can shorten your life. This is a difficult chore for many of us, but you must work on this. If you can't manage three healthy meals a day, do the best you can. The goal is always to eat healthy and avoid high-sugar and high-caffeine snacks. Okay, I can see you rolling your eyes but you know I'm right. Try eating snacks that are low sugar, low salt, and whole grain. Fresh fruit and fresh-squeezed fruit juice are always sweet-tasting healthy choices.

Working on your health every day is a wonderful investment in you. It will make you smarter and more energetic. It will improve your ability to work hard. It will give you what it takes to climb higher and higher up the mountain of success.

Faith, Conscience, and Meditation

We are all looking for meaning in life. We want to find where we fit in. We want to know our purpose and how we relate to other people, animals, and even the planet Earth. Faith, conscience, and meditation can improve your quality of life and your understanding of your place in the world. You have already rejected the notion that you are a victim. You are responsible for your actions, your life. Whatever seems unfair to you is that way because you have not taken action to change it. The world changes for better or worse one person at a time.

So, how does faith make the world better? Well, faith is the belief in something unseen. It is closely linked to hopes and dreams. With faith you reach beyond yourself for support. Most people believe in a higher power. Though I am not specifically agreeing or disagreeing with any religion, I will say that you can gain strength and calm when you reach outside of yourself. It matters that you appreciate your relationship with others and with nature. People are phenomenal creatures in a wondrous world. And we are caretakers of our world. By believing in the shared awesomeness of all things, you begin to appreciate the beauty in the world around us.

Your conscience is your sense of right and wrong. When we are totally self-centered, our conscience is minimal. If you open your heart in faith, you become empathetic to all things. Your conscience can be in tune or out of tune like an instrument. When you do wrong things or only see the negative side of things, you just add to the background noise level in the world. Your life is not in harmony. Your life is without musical melody and rhythm. Your unique life's song is a pattern of mostly high and some low notes. This melody is strengthened and guided along by a constant drumming rhythm, like a heartbeat. The song that is your life falls flat when apathy sets in or becomes sharp when you are in conflict. Your goal should be to reach harmony.

One way to reach a state of harmony is through meditation. Take twenty to thirty minutes every day to relax your mind. This does not mean to relax playing video games, talking on the phone, or watching television. These are distractions, not meditation. When I say meditation, I am referring to sitting in a chair or on a cushion with your eyes closed and breathing slowly in and out while you try to concentrate on one thing, such as a happy encounter or a goal. In time, as you become proficient at this, you will feel recharged after your meditation. A long walk in a safe area can relax you and clear your head as well. Both quiet meditation and walking can help you focus on important tasks at hand. They can give you perspective.

Faith, conscience, and meditation can assist you in improving your life and moving forward. Believe in yourself and trust that you are here on this earth to accomplish terrific things.

Time for Others

As I discussed earlier, your life is more wonderful when you are able to include others. Giving of your time to a family member, friend, or someone in need teaches you empathy and patience. It is important to walk in the other person's shoes to more clearly understand your place in this world. Understanding others is a vital part of your ongoing education. Contributing to the greater good benefits not only you but also those you help. It can assist others who are looking for their place in this world. Yes, your helpful deeds—the fact that you make an effort to reach out to others—can also inspire those around you. What's not to like about being an inspiration? Just as you are quick to copy the actions and values of adults in your life, your conduct can positively affect those looking at you. Yes, you too can be a role model or a mentor.

Take the time to get out of your shell. Reach out, because it is both socially commendable and beneficial for your mental health as well. Troubled or depressed people are not able to share their time. They are very self-focused. This is not the natural order of things. People are social creatures. When you deviate from that, you can lose touch not only with people but with your values as well. If you are not around people of other genders, races, or religions you are in a type of isolation that limits your ability to live life fully. Find the time to share your life with others. I guarantee you'll like it.

List five key points you want to remember in this chapter:

1.

2.

3.

4.

5.

Projects

1. Keep a journal of quiet times spent where you reflected on your life.

2. Volunteer to be the leader in school, church, or after-school activity.

3. Make a budget for yourself, listing what your parents spend to support you as well as any money you make (include your allowance and any part-time work). Are you on budget, over, or under? What can you do if you are over?

4. Join your parents in activities, church, fishing, camping, or any other family activity.

Suggested Reading

What Color Is My World?: The Lost History of African American Inventors by Kareem Abdul-Jabar

Chapter 9

YOUR FUTURE

Profile: Dawn Loggins

About Dawn

In simple terms, your future is up to you. Your dreams and goals, and what you do to achieve them will determine where you end up. The list of things that can distract you or slow you down is long. Life day to day can be difficult, but it still boils down to what choices you make. Dawn Loggins is a wonderful example of what dreams, goal setting, motivation, and hard work can accomplish. Her story can bring tears to your eyes; it is so hard to believe. It is inspiring that someone with so many hardships could achieve so much success. Her life is a lesson in patience, hope, and the goodness of others willing to help. Most of us have not suffered the heartbreak Dawn has lived through. It's amazing that Dawn's heart is not filled with bitterness and hate, but hope of a better life serving humankind. Here is her story.

Dawn Loggins was born in poverty in or near Lawndale, North Carolina. Her parents struggled with drug abuse, which meant that they moved often as they were kicked out of houses. It also meant that when they did have shelter, there were many times when they did not have running water or electricity. At times Dawn and her brother would have to study by candlelight, if there was money for candles or someone gave them some. Dawn and her brother would go to a local park to fetch bath, drinking, and cooking water in old milk containers.

They also lived with their grandmother for many years, because their parents could not take care of them. Living conditions with their grandmother were filthy and sparse. Dawn's whole family knew nothing but poverty and hardship. Yet she remained an A student—even though she was teased very badly by other students who knew she had not taken a bath or changed her clothes in weeks. Being different in school is bad enough, but to be terribly poor makes you more of target; some kids cannot seem to help being mean.

Dawn was lucky enough to attend Burns High School for tenth to twelfth grade. Her school guidance counselor and other staff members helped her a great deal. At one point, Dawn found herself homeless when her grandmother lost her house and her parents simply moved to Tennessee without her. They did not tell Dawn they were moving; she found out when she called home and found the phone had been disconnected. Dawn lived with friends for a while, and her brother went off on his own. Luckily, one of the school staff allowed Dawn to move in with her. She also got her a job as an assistant janitor at the school.

Most young people would not be able to remain focused on school with so many hurtful experiences. Dawn proved to be an exception. She never missed a step in school, not only getting A's but also going to honors and advanced courses. With the help of her guidance counselor, she applied to three colleges in North Carolina and one in Massachusetts. She was accepted by that world-renowned college in Cambridge, Massachusetts—Harvard University. This was a million-to-one opportunity and is the college of her dreams. Throughout her life, Dawn believed that her only way out of poverty was to get the best education. Her dream is coming true.

Job, Career, Vocation

When you dream of your future, what do you see? Are you working doing something that really makes you happy? Does your work pay well and allow you to buy things you need for your family? In your dream of the future, is the work you do a job, career, or vocation?

A job is something you do to survive; a career is the next step up. For example, working as a waiter is a job, while owning a restaurant is a career choice. Generally careers involve some post-high school education and a long-term commitment. Careers also pay considerably more than regular jobs. So, for the sake of long-term planning, if you intend to own a home, if you plan on buying a nice new car every six to eight years, and if you plan on saving money for the future, chances are you need a career. I suggest you plan accordingly.

So, what's the difference between a career and a vocation? Well, there is a small but significant difference. A vocation is work that is perfect for you. It is your calling. It could be work as a mechanic, teacher, or surgeon. It is what you are truly best at and what makes you feel like you are fulfilling your purpose. A lot of people find their vocation. They are the ones smiling as they get ready to go to work. People with a career may smile, especially on payday. And those with jobs may smile but it probably has very little to do with their work. Most people with regular jobs long for something more.

My advice to you is to "shoot for the moon." Go after your dreams. Even if you fall short of perfection, you've surpassed the regret of not having tried. You also have the satisfaction of knowing that you went after your dreams. I said before that life isn't all or nothing. Do your best, and you can hold your head up. But always do what is right for you.

What Are You Good At?

So, you want a career or vocation. An important point to remember, before we continue, is that you can be whatever you are meant to be. How then, do you figure out what that is? Well, one easy way is to make a list, in priority order, of all the things you enjoy. Make a second list, also in order, of all the things you do well. Now starting form the top of each list try to match things you Enjoy and things you Do Well. Where you find a match you have a potential career choice. As you are looking for matches it is not necessary to have a perfect fit. We are just making a first general assessment. So give yourself a little latitude and enjoy the process. Remember, you are not comparing yourself with anyone else.

Another area to look at is what your teachers have said about you over the years. The bad stuff matters, but for this exercise, concentrate on the compliments. Teachers make every effort to find something positive about every student. Even if you think a teacher didn't like you, chances he or she said something nice about you at some point.

Also while you're looking at old report cards and assessments, identify your top 2-3 subjects. Look for consistency, subjects where year after year you have done well. By well I don't necessarily mean an A but whatever your highest grades have been. This basic method can also give you a ball park estimate of what you are good at.

However, if after all of this, you still have two or three things you do well or enjoy that are about equal, it means you potentially have more strengths than most people. It may also mean that you could be happy doing several different vocations. This is still a wonderful thing. All is not lost.

What Are Your Options?

Now that you know what one to three subjects you're good at, it's time to do some research. Here you'll need Internet access. If you do not have a computer or smart phone, there are several alternatives. Try your school library, the public library, or even the YMCA. There may be other locations in and around your neighborhood.

On your computer, type in the web address **www.bls.gov/k12.** This will take you to a Department of Labor website. When you get there, the page should include the picture below.

(accessed on January 28, 2012)

This website is made specifically for fourth- through eighth-graders. Don't worry if you're younger or older. If you can read the information, you can use the site. You'll see below that the Bureau of Labor Statistics (BLS) has mapped different subjects to general career categories and even specific careers. Explore this on the website; read about the various opportunities that match your strengths and interests.

Math	Reading	Science
Statistician	Writer	Chemist
Electrical engineer	Desktop publisher	Pharmacist
Surveyor	Secretary	Pilot
Physicist	Librarian	Environmental scientist
Cost Estimator	Reporter	Engineering technician
Actuary		

Helping People	Computers	Law
Teacher	Database administrator	Police officer
Childcare worker	Computer support specialist	Lawyer
Firefighter	Computer hardware engineer	Court reporter
Nurse	Computer software engineer	Judge
Social Worker	Webmaster	Paralegal
Doctor	Systems analyst	

Social Studies	Music & Arts	Building & Fixing Things
Economist	Actor	Carpenter
Human resources assistant	Photographer	Automotive mechanic
Politician	Artist	Drafter
Psychologist	Disc jockey	Architect
Urban planner	Designer	Civil engineer
	Musician	Electrician

Managing Money	Sports	Nature
Accountant	Dancer	Zookeeper
Financial analyst	Professional athlete	Landscape architect
Loan officer	Coach	Farmer
Bookkeeping clerk	Recreation and fitness worker	Veterinarian
Real estate agent	Recreational therapist	Agricultural and food scientist

(chart accessed and simplified on January 28, 2012, from the BLS)

The information you are looking at is updated every two years by the BLS. This information is part of a bigger document called the Occupational Outlook Handbook. You can find a paper copy of this, minus the student section, which is online only, at your library. Here are some of the details you can learn about the more than eight hundred careers currently available:

- The **Significant Points** section highlights the most important occupational characteristics.

- The **Nature of the Work** section describes typical job duties and work environment.

- The **Training, Other Qualifications, and Advancement** section describes the education and training generally required to enter the occupation, as well as advancement opportunities.

- The **Employment** section gives the total number of jobs in the occupation and sometimes describes the industries, states, or occupational specialties that offer the most jobs.

- The **Job Outlook** section describes the forecast of jobs in the occupation that should be available in the future.

- The **Earnings** section provides statistics on average earnings and earnings of workers in the top 10 percent and bottom 10 percent.

- The **Related Occupations** section lists other occupations in the Handbook that have similar job duties or other characteristics.

There is a **gold** mine of information that you can find on this site. Though money should not be your sole purpose for pursuing a given career, it is an important factor. What should be obvious is that certain job groups pay more and that there is a connection between pay and education. Generally, college or technical/trade school graduates make more money than high school graduates, and high school graduates make more than high school dropouts.

How Do You Get There?

Working your options is important. Early decisions about what occupation group you prefer is also major step.

The next step is to work on the basics: reading, writing, science, and math. You have to be strong in the basics to pursue a college education. Actually, if you don't know the basics, you will struggle even in middle school. The information you learned in elementary school was foundational. Like a high-rise building, your foundation—in the basics–must be strong. In middle school, you will build on this knowledge. If you do not have that solid foundation going forward, by high school your building of knowledge will have serious cracks and could collapse.

How do you keep that from happening? Well, I will discuss this in greater detail as you proceed through this book. I will map out the path that you should take to get to your goal.

Make Weak Areas Stronger

Let's take a look at those areas where you believe that you are weak. I said before that in elementary school and beyond you can achieve high grades in all your subjects. The material may seem difficult, but before you give up, let's see what you can do. Think again about how much time and effort you can put into practicing a sport so you can play better. Though you may not end up in the WNBA or NFL, you can definitely improve your game. For some this could mean playing high school sports and possibly varsity. For a few it could mean playing sports in college or even getting a scholarship.

Just think, you have a 12 percent chance of becoming a doctor and less than a 1 percent chance of becoming a professional athlete. Pause for a moment and let that sink in. If you devote more time to study, you could have an awesome career.

So, give your study the same level of effort you give to your favorite pastime. First, you can improve your performance in nearly anything with practice. Second, even though you may not become number one, you can become stronger. In my opinion, your average grade can at least be a B.

What you consider achievable or acceptable is a function of your confidence in yourself. If you are weighed down by the anchor of low expectations, you'll drown in self-pity. Buoy yourself with great expectation for your life.

I also mentioned identifying the study method that works best for you. Try the Kahn Academy. Write things down, make your own flash cards, study with friends, or find your quiet place. You can find a project that explains a concept you want to learn. Build something or draw it. Whatever works for you, do it. Apply it to your weak areas. The more you practice, the more you will learn. So get going!

How Long Will It Take?

You may be asking, "How long will it take to get there?" The answer is, "How long have you got?" Depending on what you want to achieve and how hard you are willing to work, you can construct a timeline. For each of us, that timeline will be slightly different. And that's okay; it's normal. There's always time to succeed.

To achieve your best life—your dreams—you need to take as long as it takes. Like a roller-coaster ride, your life may take you places you never dreamed and leave you with a smile from ear to ear. Even with the ups and downs, twists and turns, you will still end up at your destination. Life's all about the journey!

List five key points you want to remember from this chapter:

1.

2.

3.

4.

5.

Projects

1. Look for and review the most recent version of one of the following career guides:

    - Occupational Outlook Handbook, from the BLS

    - EZ Occupational Outlook Handbook, from JIST Publishing (This guide uses the BLS format and data, and it includes assessment charts to help you figure out the occupation that best suites you.)

2. Determine what new careers are opening up and if you are interested in any of them.

3. Decide where you want to live and what careers are available there.

4. Every three to four months, review the **www.bls.gov/ k12** website.

Suggested Reading

- *Young Person's Occupational Outlook Handbook*, JIST Publishing

- *What Color Is Your Parachute? For Teens*, 2nd edition, by Carol Christen and Richard Bolles

Chapter 10

DEVELOPING YOUR PLAN

Profile: Nicholas S. Foley

About Nicholas

In this chapter are tools and ideas to help you develop and carry out your plan. In previous chapters, I have laid the foundation with various life skills to put you in a positive frame of mind to make superior choices. This chapter provides the icing on the cake, using all you have learned to put together your best plan for your best future.

Nicholas Foley is a great example for every young person growing up with big challenges. Like Dawn Loggins and many others, he is a beacon of strength, planning, and eagerness to learn. Here is Nicholas's story.

Nicholas Foley was raised in turmoil. He was neglected as a child, beat up by his mother's boyfriend, and at times left at school when his mom did not come to pick him up. Early in his life, both his mom and his dad abandoned him. By the age of eight, he had lived in seven different households and had six different guardians. Then two wonderful things happened that changed his life: he was adopted by his aunt, and she introduced him to the Boys and Girls Club. With the adoption, Nicholas got a new start. His aunt took him to her home in Pittsburgh. Away from the bad memories and hurt feelings that he experienced for so long in Boston, he blossomed.

Nicholas found a safe haven in the Boys Club. He learned how to be a friend; he learned empathy; and he learned that he had value and endless potential. He also became a loving individual. Tomorrow was something he could look forward to and not dread. When he first saw the Boys Club building he said to himself, "I am brand-new." In the ten years since he was adopted, he has participated in many club activities, fully embracing his second chance.

In the Boys Club, Nicholas did well in several of the athletic programs, became a junior staffer and leader, participated in the robotics team, dance team, music program, and was a summer counselor. In all, he has volunteered more than 1,500 hours of community service. In his senior year in high school, Nicholas was selected to serve as president of the Sarah Heinz House Boys and Girls Club's Keystone Club. In this role he helps other young people in leadership and community service activities.

The beginning of Nicholas Foley's life was all but hopeless. Today he looks forward to college and a career as a civil engineer. That's the plan.

Time Management

You have control of your time and your actions. You can say yes or no at any point. Pay attention to how you spend your time. Set aside the appropriate time for friends, play, and study. This does not have to be rigid. After all, I'm not talking about living in boot camp. But you do need structure. Without it, your life will be a jumble. You'll just be wandering through without rhyme or reason and accomplishing very little. Random wandering does not equal victory. Purposeful actions do.

Write down or list on your device of choice the most important things you need to do today. Plan your schedule for at least a week ahead. Grow from there.

In the beginning, concentrate on keeping your word to yourself. You'll find that this makes many things a lot easier. Whether it's getting chores done or finishing school projects on time, you'll find schedules useful. You will also find that by documenting when things are due, you can avoid the last-minute nightmares as well as have the luxury of every now and then getting things done early. Give it a try. Learn by doing.

Who, What, Where—Making Schedules and Action Plans

So, now the time has come for us to put together your plan for your best future. The chart below gives you the basic considerations you need to get going. You can use this process for small tasks, such as preparing and taking tests or completing school projects, or bigger goals, such as planning which high school or college you would like to attend.

Who	This is normally you, but it can include tutors, mentors, study partners, etc.
What	This can be preparing for the next big test or science project, improving your math grade, or the things you need to do to get into college.
Where	Where will you do this task? Location matters; it may not be a good idea to study for your English test at a basketball game.
When	This is the hard part. List the things you have to do in a given day. Some things are not flexible, like stuff your mom told you to do at a specific time. Also decide which of the items is most important and list them in order.
Tools	What do you need to do this task? Do you need a book, a computer, Internet access, paper, pencil, or other supplies?

Try this technique for your daily schedule. Note that items at the bottom of your list in importance may not get done. If you have correctly worked your priorities, this should not be a problem. The things you really need to do will get done.

After you have successfully worked this out for a few days, try a week. Keep working on this just a week in advance until you are able to plan and carry out your various tasks. When you are comfortable, plan for a month or even a year. Your longer-term plans will start out with less detail than your daily schedule. In some ways, it's easier to make the long-term schedule first and work backward from there. In this way you first figure out your major goals and then work out the details of what you need to do and when.

Here are three sample schedules. Feel free to use this format or change it as you see fit to meet your needs. By reviewing these samples, you can get a general idea of what you may want to include.

- One Week Schedule (daily details of tasks over a week's time)

- Multi-Month Schedule (a schedule covering several months of events)

- Long-Range Schedule (a big picture of goals and actions; may cover several years)

One Week Schedule

Completed:

Start: 16-April-2012   Deadline: 20-April-2012

Done?	School Subjects	Due By	Notes
	English		
No	Turn in Report	4/20/12	Ask Big Brother Randy to review 4/19
	Science		
	Semester Project	4/20/12	
No	Turn in Project	4/20/12	Make sure Charles completes his part 4/16
	History		
No	Turn in Paper	4/16/12	

Multi-Month Schedule

Completed:

| Start: | 5-March-2012 | Deadline: | 20-April-2012 |

Done?	School Subjects	Due By	Notes
	English		
Yes	Read Making Good Choices	4/2/12	
No	Write Book Report	4/11/12	
No	Turn in Report	4/20/12	
	Math		
	Geometry Test	4/13/12	
No	Study Chapter 6	4/10/12	
No	Check Kahn Academy	4/11/12	
	Science		
	Semester Project	4/20/12	
Yes	Pick a Partner	3/5/12	
Yes	Pick a Topic	3/8/12	
Yes	Write Topic Paper	3/16/12	
Yes	Turn in Paper	3/23/12	
No	Research Project	4/2/12	Get Charles to finish reading his references
No	Build Project	4/11/12	
No	Turn in Project	4/20/12	
	History		
Yes	Read Chapter 9	4/10/12	
No	Write Paper Chapter 9	4/14/12	
No	Turn in Paper	4/16/12	

Long-Range Schedule

		Completed:	
Start:	5-Mar-2012	Deadline:	Apr-2019

Done?	Science Teacher	Due By	Notes
	Elementary School		
	Identify Career Goal	3/30/12	Make decision as soon as possible
	Find mentor	3/5/12	A mentor can offer you life/career advice
	Find tutor	3/9/12	Any subject where you have a B or lower
	Middle School		
	Monitor GPA	Each semester	GPA matters for college starting in the 9th grade
	Foreign Language	Grades 8-10	Many colleges require 2-3 years of a foreign language in high school
	Continue w/tutor	Each semester	
	Continue w/mentor	Each semester	
	Prepare for Calculus	Grades 7-11	You have to take years of specific math courses before you can take calculus
	4-yr. College Search	Grade 8	As applicable
	2-yr. College Search	Grade 7	As applicable
	Trade School Search	Grade 7	As applicable
	Search for Grants	Grade 8	You can use grants
	High School		
	Scholarship Search	Grade 8	There are a ton of choices; get started early
	Student Loan Search	Grade 9	How much for the college—don't forget clothes, transportation, other living expenses
	Community Activities	Grade 7-12	Many colleges want their students to be well rounded and involved in the community
	SAT/ACT Prep	10/3/18	The SAT/ACT is a 4-year college entrance tests. You need to start preparing years ahead

Post Your Schedule/Plan

Your plan should be visible—in your face—so it's always on your mind. You can post it on the refrigerator, on the wall in your bedroom, on a pad on a table, and/or as a screen saver on your computer. Whatever you have available, make use of it. The psychology of "in your face" helps you keep focused. Like basketball players who take their basketball everywhere they go, you should keep your plan with you. Make several copies of your plan and carry it in your notebook or in your pocket. Look at it every day. Update it if it needs updating. Mark off the items you achieved, and add new items when you learn of another important step you must take to reach your goal.

An business term for this is, visual queue. A clever saying that is applicable is "out of sight, out of mind." This plan is how you will achieve your dream. Langston Hughes, a famous African American writer who lived from 1902 to 1967, once wrote,

Hold fast to dreams
For if dreams die
Life is a broken-winged bird
That cannot fly.

Hold fast to dreams
For when dreams go
Life is a barren field
Frozen with snow.

Dreams and plans are serious, life-changing things. I first learned this when I was in the fifth grade and won an essay contest. The prize was a book titled *A Pictorial History of the Negro in American*, written by Hughes and Milton Meltzer. The poem "Dreams" was hand-written on the cover page of the book. I never forgot that quote. Sometimes your inspiration comes in ways you never imagine. Until you dream, you will never achieve anything.

Find Support for Your Plan

Discuss your plan with your parents, siblings, a trusted friend, a mentor, and/or a teacher. They may be able to provide guidance to help you along your path to a brighter tomorrow. They can be a wealth of knowledge, so use them. They can provide encouragement and act as a backup you can call on if you get off track. They also can hold you accountable; this helps you carry through and keep your word.

Yet keeping your word to *yourself* may be the most important thing you ever do. The simple act of being true to yourself carries over to all your relationships as well.

Always remember to use those connections to help guide you and move you forward. Believe me, even when you become a triumphant adult, your family, friends, mentors, or support group will still be important sources of wisdom. It will always be important for you to communicate with those you love and who love you.

It's okay to feel proud of your accomplishments. But don't forget that without support and love you would not have gotten as far.

Act on Your Plan

The last step in this planning process is to execute the plan. If you are doing things right, because you are constantly adding to your plan, this will be a lifelong process. You will progress from goal to goal. You will achieve greater things as a person and as a professional.

Think of the actions in your plan as a vigorous workout. A workout has a wonderful effect on your heart, just as working your plan has a wonderful effect on your life. A physical workout isn't 24/7, but simply an everyday, regular workout. It enhances your health and welfare. It means fewer injuries, a more positive self-image, less money spent on medicine, and a better quality of life throughout your life. Acting on your plan and keeping new challenges and goals is a workout for your soul. It is just as important as a physical workout—if not more so. You must dedicate yourself to this workout as long as you have the will to get up every morning.

Believe in yourself and get to work! I look forward to hearing of your many achievements.

List five key points you want to remember from this chapter:

1.

2.

3.

4.

5.

Projects

1. Either create your own planner or purchase a planner. Use the planner.

2. Review your planner weekly to update which goals were or were not accomplished. Determine if any uncompleted goals are obsolete or should be rescheduled.

3. If you underestimated your goals, develop some that are more challenging.

Suggested Reading

It Takes a Village, 10th anniversary edition, by Hillary Rodham Clinton

Photographs and Illustrations

Michelle Obama: US Federal Government/public domain, Joyce N. Boghosian, White House photographer

Kyla Ross: Creative Commons Attribution, Scott and Emer Hults Photography

Will and Jada Smith family: Creative Commons Attribution, Harry Wad Photography

Arne Duncan: US Federal Government/public domain, United States Department of Education

Jeremy Sicile-Kira: www.chantalsicile-kira.com, Epic Photojournalism

Sukyana Roy: Creative Commons Attribution, Scripps National Spelling Bee

Angela Zhang: Siemens Foundation

Umar Brimah: CBS KFVS 12 News

Dawn Loggins: CBS *This Morning Saturday*

Nicholas Foley: Boys and Girls Club of America

ABOUT THE AUTHOR

Purvis Atkinson was born in Los Angeles, where he lived until he was eighteen. Growing up, he was always a music enthusiast and avid reader; he enjoyed all kinds of music and books. As a youngster, he sang in the children's choir in church with his sister and brothers. Later he learned to play the cello, a little. He is now a guitar student.

Mr. Atkinson has had several careers. His first began when he enlisted in the navy to become a sonar technician. He served in this capacity for ten years before being selected for a commission as an electronics and communication systems officer. He served in the navy for thirty years. His tours included several assignments in Japan, a Pentagon tour, and four years at the White House Communications Agency. After retiring from the military, Mr. Atkinson worked in the corporate sector as a senior manager for seven years. Since leaving corporate life, he has pursued the career he envisioned from the time he was a sophomore in high school: he is now a writer. He is committed to writing books like this one, which teach and inspire young people.

Mr. Atkinson is married and has one daughter. He holds a Bachelor of Science degree from Excelsior College.

He can be contacted at
www.amazon.com/author/purvisatkinson.

CPSIA information can be obtained
at www.ICGtesting.com
Printed in the USA
BVHW040217031218
534627BV00021B/583/P